IT'S OK TO CRY IN THE GARDEN

From Bankruptcy to Paradise

Bob,

Thank you for all your
knowledge - sharing.

Nanditta Colbear

Nanditta Colbear

November 2014

Library of Congress Control Number: 2014915650
ISBN: Hardcover   978-1-4990-6792-7
               Softcover   978-1-4990-6793-4
               eBook   978-1-4990-6794-1

This book was printed in Canada.

Rev. date: 09/11/2014

To order additional copies of this book, contact:
Xlibris LLC
1-888-795-4274
www.Xlibris.com
Orders@Xlibris.com
656913

Contents

This book is dedicated to my late father-in-law, Al, who taught me some valuables business lessons and my mother-in-law, Ruth, who taught me how to make awesome apple pies.

For my parents, Prabha and Prem, who carted my century old bicycle featured on the cover, all the way from India.

To Sasha, our dog, whose snores keep me typing.

For Ric, my editor, my life inspiration and my partner in all things big and small.

Thank you to:

Steve Hardy for reading the manuscript as it evolved and for the book's title.

Howie Longfellow for the cover picture.

Wayne F. LeBelle for his persistent, "Have you finished the book yet?"

Readers of my weekly column for their communications; all the horticultural societies for inviting me to speak to their membership and encouraging me to write my first book.

REFLECTIONS

I sat in the all glass sunroom, enjoying a steaming cup of tea. The sun had been up for just a short while and the house still quiet. The river appeared to be asleep – not one ripple marred its mirror like deep blue surface. It was my fifty-second birthday and I felt really good. A slight northerly breeze made my nose twitch as a musky scent tickled it. Following the smell, I shifted my head just a bit and saw a large moose with two young ones beside her. The mother looked directly at me, as the two calves played at the water's edge.

Careful not make any sudden movements, I continued to enjoy my morning tea in the company of the moose family. "Could you have imagined a moment like this, ten years ago?" my inner voice asked. The breeze picked up just a bit shattering the reflections of the moose on the river. "Is this a dream?" I asked myself. Delicately I sniffed the air. Ten years ago I would have smelt pollution, fumes from traffic, perfume and cigarette smoke – all the smells of downtown urban life in Toronto.

I could smell creeping thyme that grows around our house, a hint of mint and the sweet smell of some flowers. The twins kept going into the river and running back to their mother. She stood still and alert to all danger. The wind shifted and she said something to the little ones. Suddenly, all three moose disappeared into the bush, leaving me alone to finish my tea. Unexpectedly I felt a drop on my hand and I realized that I was crying. The tears marked another moment of wonder created by nature's beauty and the conviction that the past helped create this moment.

The gentle breeze soothed and relaxed me, as my mind drifted back in time. My husband Ric and I lived in downtown Toronto for many years. Our condominium was on the twentieth floor of a building on Yonge Street, just minutes from Bloor Street. Overlooking Rosedale Valley on the eastside, we had a clear view of the trains that provide easy access to the business core. Just around the corner, south of us was the busy Yorkville fire station. We were so used to the sounds of the trains, buses, traffic and the fire engines going by, that we did not notice the noise at all.

To the south east we had a clear, but distant view of Lake Ontario. In the summer it was a treat to see sailboats out on the waters. I enjoyed staring out at them, weaving tales about the people that were out on the water. The warm breeze drifting through our windows always carried the smell of hotdogs and gasoline. Riding on the breeze was the sound of trains coming into and leaving the Rosedale Valley subway station. The unique grinding noise of the train's breaks as it came to a halt and then, like clockwork, the rhythmic sound of the engine picking up speed as the train moved towards its next stop. Our lives were typical of busy urbanites with a twist.

"Happy birthday to you, happy birthday," Ric's deep melodious voice brought me back to the present day with a start. Sasha, our pretty ten year old Shih Tzu, joined in the fun with her rendition of the same song.

"Good morning love and a very happy birthday. You seemed very far away."

"I am not sure what happened here. One minute I was watching a moose family and the next minute I had drifted back a decade," I replied somewhat puzzled.

"Well get used to it – it happens a lot as you get old!"

"I have a ways to go before I claim the senior citizen discounts that you have been enjoying for a while," I retorted.

Sasha, let off a volley of barks before Ric could come back with any comments. She is normally a very quiet dog, but when she wants her next meal she is pretty vocal.

"What would you like for breakfast?" Ric asked with a smile.

"Wild blueberry pancakes, with warm butter, sausages and our local maple syrup," I said gleefully. Ric tends to spoil me a lot, but even more so on my birthdays. Every time I look at him, it surprises me how with the passage of time he gets to be more distinguished looking. Aging has been kind to his skin – mine, meanwhile, is showing more wrinkles and spots. I think it is a male thing – they age better than us.

Our dining room overlooks the river and the open space around us. From the first meal we ever shared, to this day, we like to set the table properly. Pretty napkins, placemats, proper silverware, crystal glasses and lovely china. It is our weakness, along with lovely white candles and delicious home-cooked meals. We discovered local maple syrup soon after we moved north. Even after all these years, every time we open the jug of syrup from Desjardins & Fils Sucrerie, I feel a deep sense of wonder. Their sugar bush is up the street from our home. The syrup seems just a bit more precious because of the proximity of the maple trees that give us this lovely nectar every spring.

Wild blueberries are abundant in this area. It always surprised me that we had none on our property. This summer I found a small patch at one end of our land. I cannot wait for next season to see if we get fruit on the bushes.

"So, where were you?" Ric asked.

Gulping down a mouthful of pancake I replied "In Toronto. Did you ever think we would find ourselves in a place like this?"

With a smile and a dreamy look, Ric replied. "I dreamt about it. I always knew that I would either live in the heart of the city or in the country. The suburbs were never for me. What were you thinking about, when we pulled you back to this day?"

"Uhm! A bit of this and a bit of that. Remember how we used to laugh about our lake view – that tiny strip of blue water miles away from our condo."

"Toronto served its purpose. We had a busy but good time. Besides, that's how we could afford to move here," he murmured in a soft contemplative manner.

"That's so true. Do you miss it? Any regrets?" I asked Ric.

Ric reached over and took my hand in his. Looking into his deep blue eyes, I could see the contentment even before he spoke. "None at all. I love our life and I am glad that we have been able to share so many experiences. I would not change a thing – the ups and the downs – I'd leave everything as is. Every moment, every event had its purpose."

For a while, breakfast done, we sat lost in thought, enjoying each other's company and the lovely river view. Breaking the silence, I said, "Guess it is time for me to cleanup."

"No you sit, I will cleanup."

"You made breakfast, so I get to clean," I said.

"It's your birthday and different rules apply. Relax, daydream or go bury your nose in a book."

Sasha decided it was time for her walk and took the decision out of my hands. Nothing like a nice walk after a lovely breakfast, I thought to myself. I changed into my walking shoes and the two of us went out. We have thirteen acres of land with lots of places to walk and explore.

"Come on, Sasha, keep up," I yelled as she stopped to sniff every tree. The trail we were on, heads down from the house to the lowest point on our property. There are large trees like birch, poplar and pine. The trail follows the natural curves of the river and there are trees that have come down that provide resting spots. We sat down to watch life on the river – ducks, mergansers and one lonely loon.

Sitting quietly, I can hear the wind – it sounds like incoming ocean tides. There is a soft rustle, a whooshing sound just before you feel it on the skin. Memories of Toronto come rushing back. Our lives were so hectic and fast-paced. One year we decided to start buying season's tickets to the Toronto Blue Jay's baseball games. The SkyDome, now named the Rogers Centre, proved to be the perfect place for us to slow down and enjoy a few quiet hours, with forty thousand other fans.

The Sunday games were usually in the afternoon and most times the Sky Dome roof would be open, presenting us a chance to enjoy the sun. Ric and I would take the train from Rosedale subway station to Front Street and then walk over. As we got close to the stadium mouthwatering smells of roasting hot dogs and burgers would assail our senses. We always got a hot Italian sausage on a bun from the same vendor. Over the years the owner and his wife would look for us at the start of the season. It became our tradition to stop and chat with them and say goodbye for the winter at the last game of the season.

We'd enjoy a beer and sing along to the loud music played at events like these. My favourite one was the seventh inning stretch – the cheerleaders would come out and we would all get up and follow their movements. To this day when I hear the song 'Take me to the ball game' or 'YMCA' – I have to fight the urge to jump up and dance. However, these relaxing moments were few – for the most part we worked seven days a week. Long days were dedicated to growing and expanding our business.

One day, Ric received some bad news. His friend, Adrie, died suddenly – a heart attack. "I am really sorry, honey," I said, while hanging on to his arm. We stood looking out the window of our living room. The city lights brightened the horizon – tall well-lit skyscrapers around us. We could see the steady lights of traffic and hear the distant sirens.

"Apparently, he was going to one of the grocery stores he owned. It seems that he pulled off the highway and that is how he was found – dead in the car."

"Life is short and hard to predict. Just like when Gordie died. It happened so unexpectedly. I still find it hard to believe that he is gone," Ric said, referring to another friend who passed away a few years earlier. "We need to slow down. All this will mean nothing, if we do not live to enjoy it."

"You are right my love, the pace has been superfast," I said. "Would you like a glass of wine? We could sit on the balcony for a while."

Our top floor condominium had an enclosed balcony that we had setup with nice chairs and a table. We opened the large windows and sat late into the night, lost in thought for a while.

Ric broke the silence, his face reflecting his feelings of wonder mixed with disbelief. "We have come a long way in the last five or six years. Can you believe, you were out of work and I had to declare personal bankruptcy!"

"As your dad would say – the harder I work, the luckier I get." I commented. "It is true – we have worked very hard to get to this point in our lives." With a deep sigh I added, "What are we going to do?"

Ric took a sip of the merlot and said, "We are going to have to find a way to slow down."

"We should stop going to work on the weekend," I told him.

His tone uncharacteristically sharp, Ric stated, "We say that, but then go in anyway. What we need is a second home – a cottage or something that will take us away from Toronto."

"I guess I can call Erna at the real estate office, but you know she will ask for our wish list. We will need to come up with a budget, too." I replied, giving him a knowing look.

Sasha jumped on my leg to get my attention and brought me back to reality. "What do you want, girl – do you want to get going?" It was time for us to get moving again. We headed back towards the house and then made a left turn to one of our vegetable gardens. The season was almost over and there were just a few things left to harvest. The one time our old dog shows energy is when she's nearing the vegetable patch. She loves eating peas and beans. This season we had planted a late crop of both for a fall harvest. Sasha scampered ahead of me to see if she could find a few to munch on.

Green, yellow and purple beans took on a whole new meaning once we started growing them. There is a special pleasure in walking to the garden, harvesting beans and cooking them right away. When they are this fresh it only takes minutes to cook them. We enjoy ours with a dash of butter, salt and pepper – crunchy, juicy and sweet. Standing in front of the vegetable patch, it is hard to believe that we never had a garden before we moved north.

Living in downtown Toronto we used to frequent Kensington Market (in the heart of Chinatown) – that was our source for vegetables and herbs. In the summer we would drive to the suburbs in search of farms selling their produce by the side of the road. Buying farm fresh cauliflowers, potatoes, onions, beans and peas was as close to gardening as we came. I remember like it was yesterday the discussion Ric and I had while making our 'wish list' for the real estate agent.

"I want a property on the water," I told Ric, in my really stubborn voice – a tone that said I am not compromising.

"I would like lots of land, possibly rolling hills – a real country setting," Ric said wistfully. As is often the case, our budget was small and one year into our search we found nothing we could afford. We saw some properties that we adored, but the price was well above our budget. All in all, with the passage of time, we were very sure about what we wanted.

"Nanditta, come-in. Over," the walkie-talkie in my pocket crackled. We have a strict rule in our household – neither of us wanders off without a way to communicate with the other.

"Hi, we are over in the far field – you should be able to see us from the sunroom – over."

"I see you – what would you like for dinner? Over."

"You cooking? Over."

"Still your birthday – so yes. Over." Ric replied. I could tell from his tone that he was smiling.

"I just ate some shell peas – yummy. If you make your spicy back ribs, I can make the rice and pea salad. Over."

"Sounds like a plan. Over." Ric said.

"I am picking peas, as we speak! I will swing by the herb patch for the mint and scallions. See you in a bit. Over and out." I exclaimed.

More than fifteen years ago I used to watch a show on television that was all about cottage lifestyles in the Muskoka's – beautiful homes on the lake. One time they had featured this salad – it combined cooked long grain basmati rice at room temperature with shelled sweet peas, chopped mint and scallions. It was tossed with olive oil, lemon zest and juice and a bit of salt and pepper. It is the perfect accompaniment to spicy chicken wings or back ribs. The peas add a sweet complexity to the meal. As I walked towards the herb patch, which is close to the house, but a good three hundred feet from the far field, I was drawn back into the past.

With Sasha at my heel (the peas made her very obedient), I remembered our early years together. We hit rock bottom, shortly after we fell in love. Through sheer bad luck Ric had made a series of bad investments. The magnitude of his financial losses became clear over time. Not just him, but some of his business associates were victims of a fraudulent scheme – something to do with orange groves in Costa Rica. While he tried to get a handle on the disaster, I got the proverbial 'pink-slip' – a notice of department closure and job loss.

I have always enjoyed romantic movies and novels. Love always seems like this wondrous feeling of belonging and joy. What the books never described for me was the depth of sharing that love embodies — feeling your lover's despair, sharing the hopelessness and self-doubt. Through those very dark days I learned that one can communicate without words, find strength in weakness and silence can provide inspiration. Two halves that complement, complete and create one whole. Barbara Cartland style fairy-tale romances that I enjoyed a lot as a young girl had nothing in common with the reality we faced.

Romance was walking miles through the downtown core on a cold snowy day to get cheap groceries. We had large backpacks that we'd strap on to our backs and walk to Chinatown, about five kilometres from our place. We would walk back with our packs full of food, having spent just a few dollars. We became part of the fabric of Kensington Market.

Ric got to know the people at European Meats – a lovely old style store where we purchased all our meats. They would throw in a few juicy meat bones – perfect for making soups. While he was buying the meats, I'd buy vegetables. The store was just down the street and for about six dollars I would walk out with four full grocery bags – fruits, herbs and vegetables. Every few weeks, we'd pick up a carton of eggs at the 'egg lady's store.' She really liked Ric and they would chat for a bit. She introduced us to quail and turkey eggs. Finally, there was the cheese store. As soon as we'd walk in free samples would come our way – variety of cheeses – those on special, those that were new, creamy ones, hard ones. The owners would give us samples on tiny pieces of bread. This was our special treat, before we headed back home.

Romance was in sharing a sausage on a bun at European Meats or getting freshly baked buns at the bakery and eating it with cheese, right outside the store. We worried together – how to pay bills, where will the next meal come from, what will tomorrow bring? We helped each other through the dark phase, finding optimism in moments that held no promise and promising each other we would never give up – as long as we were a team. Poverty, hunger and despair can either make or break a relationship. Hopelessness is corrosive and will eat through the strongest material. Love, trust and faith are the only antidotes.

The familiar smell of thyme filled my senses – aromatic, fresh, pungent and distinctive. I planted creeping thyme seeds around the house the year we moved up from Toronto. It has spread, threading its way through grass and weed. At the height of the summer, it has pale lavender blossoms that the bees adore. I know I have reached home as soon as I step on this beautiful carpet of perfection – a few seeds planted without any thought, became a symbol of homecoming. A home that we found by chance – a few strokes on a keyboard on a cold wintery evening led us to this paradise we call Kashmir Acres.

CHANCE OR DESTINY?

"Have a good evening, Nanditta. Are you planning to work well into the night?"

"Oh John, you startled me. Nazee from San Francisco called earlier today and said she was running late for a meeting, but needed to speak to me about the person we had interviewed for the Front Desk Manager position, today. I am waiting for her to call back – the three hour time difference does not help. Has everyone left?"

"Yes, you were on the phone for a while there, when the main shift ended. Would you like me to lock the door behind me?" he asked, as he prepared to leave for the day.

"That would be great and thank you John, it was a good day – great job handling the Houston interview. Oh! Tonight's your regular curling night is it not?"

"Yes, I am headed to the club."

"Good curling, see you in the morning."

'Good night," John called out as he headed out.

I left my office and walked out to the main staff space that overlooked Yonge Street. We had an open concept office, with custom made cubicles for all the staff. The east wall of the office was all windows that allowed lovely natural light throughout the day for the staff to enjoy. The city lights were muted by the falling snow. It had been cold over the last few days and looking out at the snow, I was sure we would have a white Christmas – just over three weeks left in the year, I thought.

As we had for some years, we would spend Christmas with my in-laws in Fonthill. Ric and I had been cooking the traditional dinner for the family. A few years back his mother had to undergo some surgery and that year we made the dinner. I guess everyone enjoyed it enough that we have been doing so ever since. I reminded myself to call the car rental agency to reconfirm our reservation. Ric NEVER drives his delicate old Mercedes Benz in the winter. The salt is not good for her, according to him. Apparently, she was made in a country where they do not salt the roads. The car has a reserved spot in the building basement and has to be kept covered at all times, so the dust does not bother her delicate sensibilities. For crying out loud, it is a 1970 model car – younger than me, yet it gets more attention than I do.

I think I will wait one more hour for the client to call and if she has not, I am heading out, I thought with a big yawn. It has been a long day. I decided to surf the Internet for a while. For the past year or more I perused the MLS listings every week. Our real estate agent had got me into checking for cottages on a regular basis. Sometimes, for the fun of it I would look at properties in British Columbia and compare them to the ones available in the east coast – huge price difference. In fact, there were some really affordable cottages in Nova Scotia – too bad it was so far away.

Once I made my way to the MLS listing website, I started the search as always looking in the Niagara region. We figured that was a good spot for us, as we would be close to Ric's family. Usually, I would start near Niagara-on-the-Lake and start making my way back towards Toronto – searching in various regions along the way. For the most part, properties in our budget had no land or no water frontage.

"Good evening Compu-Skrēn Communications, Nanditta speaking, how may I assist you?" I answered the phone using my professional voice.

"It's Ric, are you coming home?"

"I am waiting for Nazee from San Francisco to call, its only 4:00 pm there. I will wait another half hour and try calling her."

"OK – dinner is ready. See you soon." Ric said as he hung up.

Our office used to be on Bay Street between Yorkville and Scollard Avenues. Just over a year ago, we outgrew the space on Bay as our business expanded. Tonight I was glad of the short commute the new location provided us. The building to which we relocated is a bit unique. The bottom ten floors are commercial and the top ten are residential. Our office was on the eighth floor of the building and our condominium on the top floor.

I walked over to the windows and it was still snowing. I took one last peek at the real estate listings – this time focusing on the Hamilton-Burlington region.

"What!" I yelled, "It cannot be – there has to be a mistake." I looked at the computer screen again, blinked and looked again. It's just not possible, I thought.

I pushed line one on the phone and hit speed dial three. The phone rang and rang, finally a person picked up. "Please may I speak with Erna?"

"The office is closed – this is the answering service. May I take a message?"

"Will you be letting Erna know that I called, right away," I asked.

"Yes, the agents get paged and know they have a message waiting. However, she may not respond until tomorrow," the voice replied.

"OK – I get it, please tell her Nanditta called and I am at the office for a few minutes longer or she can call us at home. She has both our numbers. Thank you very much and have a great evening."

Patience has never been my strong suit and this evening was no different. I looked at my watch, impatiently, paced and waited for the phone to ring. Even though not a minute had passed since I left the message, it felt like hours. Please, please call, I thought. "With my luck, Nazee will call and I will end up missing Erna's call," I thought. Maybe I should call Ric and alert him to the possibility of Erna's call. "No, no, don't call – what if she calls while you are on the phone." My inner dialogue was interrupted by the shrill ringing of the phone. It could be Nazee, I thought as I mechanically furnished the professional business greeting.

"Hi Nanditta, its Erna – you called?"

"Erna, I am delighted you called me – thank you, thank you!" I yelled excitedly. "Where is Sturgeon River?"

"Uhm – sounds familiar- my brother lives near a Sturgeon River or lake. It's just north – in the Muskokas, I think. Why?"

"Are you near your computer?" I asked.

"No, I am not at home."

"Erna, I found this property on the Sturgeon River – it is just perfect for us. It has thirteen acres of land and more than two thousand feet of waterfront and it is within our budget – actually, lower than our budget!" I yelled, jumping up and down.

"There has to be a mistake – they probably missed a few zeros in the price," Erna said. "Who is the listing agent?" she demanded.

"It is your agency's Hamilton office." I cried with excitement.

"Nanditta, calm down – it is probably a mistake – I am sure the price is incorrect. It must be a new listing. Listen, give me the MLS number and I will call the agent in the morning."

"What if it sells by the morning? Oh Erna, can you call now, please?"

"Nothing sells that easily – go home, rest and I will call you tomorrow morning. Will you be at work early?"

"Ric will be here ahead of me, but I should be in well before nine. Thank you Erna."

"Good night Nanditta – and go home," she exclaimed as she disconnected.

I turned off the computer and decided not to call the client in San Francisco. On my way out, I made sure all the fax machines had paper and were online. Next I turned off the lights and then set the security alarm. I ran to the elevator and punched the 'down' button a few times. The building is old and the elevators take a long time. Finally, I heard the ping as it came to halt on my floor and the doors opened. I rushed in and pushed the button to the basement 'level one.' For security reasons, the office section of the building has its own elevators. We can go to the lobby, exit through the main doors and then enter the building from another set of doors to access the residential area. Alternately, we can take the office elevators to the basement and then using our special security pass, enter the residential side.

I did not want to step out into the snow at all and made my way to the residential elevators through the cold basement. "Geez, can you be any slower," I thought as I waited impatiently for the elevator. The ride up to the twentieth floor took forever, but I was finally home. I banged on our door until Ric opened it, "Did you forget your keys?"

"No, I was in a hurry to get inside!" I exclaimed, bouncing around like a boxer.

"That hungry. Would you like a glass of wine before we eat?" he asked with a welcoming smile.

"Yes. No. I mean where is the Sturgeon River?"

"Relax. Here take a sip of this wine and tell me what is going on?"

"Well, do you know where it is?" I demanded, as I gulped down some excellent Verdichio. Ric is my 'go-to' guy for all things Canadian.

"I think it is way up north – near Sudbury or North Bay, I think? The name rings a bell."

"What!" I shrieked, "It cannot be. Erna thinks it is just north of Toronto."

"What's going on – why are you getting upset?" Ric asked in his most soothing tone.

"Well, I found this place, its perfect and now you are saying it is at the other end of the world. Of course I am upset." I wailed.

"North Bay is not – never mind. Sit, start at the very beginning and tell me what is going on," Ric demanded as he went and turned the burners down on the stove.

It took me a few minutes to compose myself. My heart was thudding so hard, I could hear it above the soft music playing in the background. Ric came and sat down beside me, waiting patiently for me to tell the story. Stumbling a bit, I finally settled down enough to recap my findings.

"I am pretty sure that there is a Sturgeon River near North Bay. Here, let me get our Ontario atlas out." Ric said, as he went to look for the book.

I felt so disappointed, I could cry. I was sure I had found 'the place' for us. I hope he is wrong, I thought to myself. I bet it is just north of Toronto, like Erna said. On the other hand, most of the properties in the rich Muskoka region, that I had researched, were worth millions. Maybe this is just an undiscovered area.

"Here we are," Ric's voice interrupted my musings. We looked under 'S' in the back of the book and sure enough, there was a Sturgeon River listed. Much to my dismay, it was indeed near North Bay.

Dinner was a quiet affair, as I dealt with my disappointment. I felt like the prize had been pulled out from under my nose. One minute I had made the discovery of a lifetime, only to find out that my diamond was a piece of coal.

Out of necessity, as we had only one bathroom, one of us was ready before the other. Usually this meant that the first one ready headed to work and opened up. I followed shortly after, with fresh home brewed coffee in travel mugs – one of the luxuries of living in the same building. I know that the proximity to work made it that much easier to work long hours but I especially enjoyed the ability to go home for lunch.

The intercom buzzed at my desk, "Nanditta, Erna is on line three. She says you are expecting her call."

"Thank you Kat, I will take the call."

"Good morning Erna, how are you today?" I chimed in, trying to be positive.

"Cold and snowed in – I am working from home. I have good news and bad news, which would you like first." Erna asked ruefully.

"The bad, I guess." I knew I sounded deflated, but there was not much I could do as disappointment overwhelmed me.

"The property is way north. It is near Sturgeon Falls, on the other side of North Bay."

"I know – that is what Ric told me. What's the good news?"

Sounding optimistic she said, "It is still on the market and the price is correct. However, the owner is also advertising it as a rental and it sounds like he may have some bites. The agent suggested that if we are interested we should make a move. What do you think?"

Feeling a deep regret and knowing that sometimes it is best to let go, I said in a matter-of-fact-voice, "No Erna, it is seven hundred kilometers in the wrong direction. We were looking to be close Ric's parents. Anyway, thank you very much for jumping on this. Stay warm."

"Say hi to Ric and have a great day. Bye."

Ric's office is next to mine – however, to access it, I had to step into the main office. The staff were all at their desks and I could hear the muted sounds of our normal workday. The business had grown rapidly and we were now employing twenty five people.

"Got a moment?" I asked, stepping into Ric's domain.

"Sure, I am just finishing up on a few loose ends – what's up?"

"Erna called, you were right – the property is too far north. She is going to call the agent and let them know that we are not interested." My tone was resigned and my manner dejected.

"OK. What is the work load like for the day?"

"Typical for this time of year – it is slowing down. Everyone has interviews today, so that is good. I still have to get a hold of Nazee and there were a few client calls overnight."

"How are you feeling?" Ric murmured.

"I am fine with it – I just had such high hopes. Anyway, it is what it is!"

Back in my office, I tried to focus on work and not think about real estate. One of our biggest challenges, in business, was managing the time zones. We had clients across North America, spanning all the time zones. Shift work, time-management and some creative scheduling got us through most of the issues. As the year neared its end, we were likely to see a bit of a slowdown. Usually, this was a time where I could catch up on administrative details, accounting and paperwork.

Today, though, I felt restless and unable to focus. I was contemplating going out for some cold air and a dose of snow, when Ric walked into my office.

"What if we went and looked at this property?" he said, surprising me.

"Why? It is so far away, we are not going north – what's the point?" I whined.

"One of the things that has led to our business success is keeping an open mind. There are possibilities and then there are possibilities," he emphasized his comments by cutting the air with his right hand. "We always said that everyone and every idea gets a fair hearing. There is no such thing as a stupid question or idea. We will research, look at all angles before ruling something out."

"Be realistic – it is winter, this place is in the bugaboos of Canada, somewhere remote and far. Besides, the owner has someone interested in renting it out." I cried regretfully.

"Listen to me – there is a reason you stumbled upon it. Let's take a break, it is slowing down. John can handle the business for a few days. We could make it our vacation," Ric said with a big smile.

"Seriously – how would we get there? Where is North Bay, anyway?" I whined.

"We could rent a four-wheel drive vehicle and make it an adventure!"

"I don't know, honey. I told Erna to tell them we are not interested and we are scheduled to be at your parent's place for Christmas."

"Call Erna, talk to her! Christmas is still two weeks away."

Sometimes when Ric gets all excited about an idea, he is irresistible. His eyes get this sparkle and he looks like a kid about to open a Christmas present. So I called Erna. As it turned out, she knows us well. She had not called the other agent back. She felt we should pick a date finalize our plans within the next hour and get back to her with a travel date. Then, she would call the agent.

"I think you should plan to be there within the next day or so," were her last words to me.

Feeling energized, I called the car rental place in our building and managed to snag a Ford Explorer for two days. Next up I completed an Internet search for a hotel in North Bay and found a Travelodge on Lakeshore Drive. I called them and was able to get us a room for the night in question. Next, I called Erna and provided her with our itinerary. She was going to call the agent and iron out some details. Now back to the waiting game.

It was a bitterly cold day – the sun was shining and we were headed north. Getting out of the city took forever – traffic, congestion, typical downtown Toronto. Eventually we made our way to Highway 400, cranked up the music and headed towards our adventure. Ric seemed very comfortable behind the wheel and looked pretty excited about the prospect of going to North Bay. I did not drive and that meant the burden was on him. I had the Ontario map open, so I could navigate.

We made one pit stop and one lunch stop along the way. Once we were on Highway 11, there was hardly any traffic. The snow banks were pristine clean and white. I was astounded at how white the snow was – we had become accustomed to the dirty brown tones of urban snow – pollution has a way of affecting everything.

"Look how blue the sky is?" I exclaimed.

"We are gonna have a party, a party for two," Ric and I sang along with Shania.

Finally, we were at the hotel in North Bay and the temperature was a balmy "minus" twenty seven Celsius. We had directions to this property in a place called Field. The owner's friend was to meet us at the house and show us around. Ric had anticipated the "cold" and we had packed our cold weather coats and ski-pants that were seldom used in Toronto. The plan was to check-in at the hotel, change into warmer clothes and then head out.

About an hour later, we drove through a tiny village named Sturgeon Falls. Following the real estate agent's directions, we turned north on Highway 64.

"I hope we are there soon," Ric fretted. "It is starting to get a bit dark."

"You are sure this is the right way?" I asked a few minutes later, "There is nothing around. I have not seen any houses or lights for a bit."

"I am following their directions. Let us go up a few more minutes and if we see nothing, we will turn around."

I was starting to feel a bit of panic. There had been no traffic – no vehicles behind us and the light was starting to fade.

"I think we should turn around, Ric, this does not look good." I implored.

Ric kept driving in silence. What felt like an eternity, but was only a few more minutes, Ric said, "Anytime now. They had said the house is on the right and the owner's friend, Ron will meet us on the highway. We should see a car soon."

"There, there," I yelled and pointed at a vehicle pulled to the side of the road. Ric signaled and slowed down. Sure enough – we had reached our destination.

A few hours later we were back at the hotel, chilled to the bone and hungry.

"What did you think?"

"I am not sure, at all. It was small, cold, dark, damp and dingy. The dead mice did not help things at all." I replied scrunching my nose. Even though we were back in North Bay, the odd smell in the house had not left me – I could still smell the stale damp air.

"Remember, we had talked about not worrying about the condition of the house. We had said we would consider the property as a whole. Let us see how we feel when we go back tomorrow morning and walk around the place. Okay?"

"Hmm. What's for dinner?" I said, changing the subject.

We ended up going to a nearby restaurant that the hotel front desk agent recommended. Both of us were really surprised that the restaurant had a smoking section and we could smell the smoke. Toronto had banned smoking in public places a while back and we were not used to the smoke. Through dinner we talked about our trip to Field. Nights in Toronto are always so bright – buildings, street lights, neon signs – all contribute to well-lit nights. The first thing both of us talked about was the absolute dark in sections of the drive between Field and North Bay. Highway 64 has no lights, at all. In contrast the snow was pure white – the word 'pristine' took on a new meaning.

We were up really early the next day – it was a clear, cold morning. The drive to Field seemed to go much faster this time. Ron, the owner's friend, had told us which direction to head upon our return during the day. For the record, it was minus 29 Celsius that day. The snow was so deep I was sinking almost to my hip. Ric had nice ski boots from the time he went on a downhill skiing trip to the Rockies. All I had on were ankle high fancy hiking boots. Before long, I was out of breath and unable to keep up with Ric.

Finally, Ric came up with a plan – he shortened his stride, so I could I walk in his footsteps. It worked! We walked forever – I calculated that it was a few city blocks when we finally came to a stop. We could see the little blue house on the hill from where we stood. Neither of us could fathom that all this land came with the house.

"How wide is the river?" I asked Ric.

"Hard to say – everything is snow covered, but it looks like a fair size."

"Do you think it would be about ten feet wide?"

"Oh, it is much more than that!" Ric exclaimed. "Look to that far side – I think that is the opposite bank – there, by the trees," he pointed.

"Wow! Really?"

We stood in silence in the cold for a while. Each lost in their own thoughts. Eventually, it was time to head back to Toronto, with a quick breakfast break in North Bay.

An Elephant

"How cold is it?" I asked Ric.

"About minus twenty five," he replied, looking through the window at the outside thermometer.

Feeling energized, I said, "I think I will strap on the snowshoes and head out for a bit. It is not that windy, should not be so bad on the trail. Think about tonight's dinner menu, while I am gone!" This winter there had been a lot of snow and every time we had our snowshoe trails packed down to make walking comfortable, we'd get another dumping of snow.

"Make sure you have your ski pants on," Ric admonished, "The wind has picked up and don't forget the walkie-talkie."

"Nag, nag, nag," I muttered under my breath, as I went back into the living room to get the forgotten walkie-talkie. It was not long before I hit the trail, thankful for the ski pants and the thick coat as the wind swept up from the river. From the house, the trail heads east towards the river. The forested area is to the right and the river to the left. Throughout the winter, beaver make their way to the forest, chew down saplings and drag them toward the river.

Despite the cold northerly wind, I find being outdoors exhilarating - the air crisp, fresh and full of promise. I enjoy looking at the animal tracks in the snow and making up stories in my head. It is rare for me to identify all the tracks correctly, but it is fun to pretend I know. I feel like a pioneer woman out hunting and gathering for her family.

Along the trail, I have my favourite rest stops, where I pause and look back at our house. I know Ric probably has the binoculars out, checking on my progress. Now and then I can hear the chickadees singing in the forest. The Blue Jays tend to fly just ahead of me, keeping an eye on things. They act like they are hiding something from me.

A bit tired I tried to pick up the pace as the wind was getting to me. My eyes were watering and my glasses fogging up. Just before I get to the turnaround point, where we have our dock in the summer, there is a natural pond. During the warmer months ducks, frogs and other living creatures use it as their personal hangout.

To the left of the trail, beside the pond, are some wild highbush cranberry trees. The berries are small, bright orange and have a large inedible seed in the middle. These berries are quite tart before the cold weather and fall frosts arrive. After that they are tangy with a sweet finish. We gather several bags of the wild berries and make jelly that lasts us until the next season. We always leave plenty on the branches for the birds and I.

As always, I stopped to enjoy some frozen berries. It is the perfect treat while taking a break from snowshoeing. These tiny berries are hard to pick with the thick gloves on my hands. But if I take the gloves off, my fingers get painfully cold. I discovered that the branches are very pliable.

Usually, I pull a berry laden branch close to my face and grab a few with my teeth. It is incredible – the frozen berry hits the warm mouth and before long I am enjoying nature's nectar.

"Ouch!" A sharp twig scratched my cheek as I tried to guide the berries to my mouth. I flinched and my hand snapped off the stem that held the berries. A few things happened at the same time. There was a loud crack and the sound of wings flapping as a huge bird flew right before my eyes. The berries fell, my ski pole slipped out of my hand and my heart skipped a beat.

I stood frozen to the spot, trying to calm down. The monstrous bird was actually a harmless partridge – inadvertently, I had disturbed its resting place by the pond. Trying to kneel on the soft snow, while wearing snowshoes is not the easiest thing. However, I was determined to find the stem that held about ten berries. Grumbling under my breath I managed to rummage around the snow until I found the tasty morsels.

As I tried to stand up, I heard a ripping sound – the old ski pants were protesting all this activity. The memories came rushing back. The ski pants were more than fifteen years old. Soon after we moved the office from Bay Street to Yonge Street, in Toronto, we realized that we were not getting much exercise. At least, before the move, we had to walk to work, every day. With the office and the condominium being the same building, we just availed of elevators.

We decided to get a membership to a health club that had opened just a block away from us. A few times a week, we'd head out for a workout. As winter set in, it became a chore. Ric and I decided we needed warmer clothes to encourage us to go to the gym on cold mornings. One weekend we took the subway south, past the Toronto Eaton Centre, to go to Mountain Equipment Co-op, a sporting goods store. We purchased heavy-duty, beautifully lined ski pants to help us with Toronto's winter.

"Come in, Nanditta. Over." Ric's voice crackled, pulling me back to the present. I was laughing so hard it took me a few seconds to reply.

"Hello. Over."

"Cannot see you, where are you? Over." Ric's tone held some anxiety.

"Just by the pond. Over."

"Are you heading back? It's been a while. Over."

"Yup, on my way. Over and out." I fumbled in my pocket, looking for the handkerchief I always carried. I could not help grinning as I dried my eyes and headed up the hill – back home. As I got close, I could smell wood smoke. Ric has the fireplace going, I thought.

I stopped, turned and glanced back at the trail, "We have come a long way in ten years. Ten scary, but wonderful years."

The fire warmed my back as I stood as close to the fireplace as I could. There is nothing better than a roaring fire to help reenergize.

"Do you remember the time we bought these ski pants?" I demanded.

With a smile, Ric said, "To go the gym in the winter."

I burst out laughing, "Yeh, it used to by minus three with a wind chill making it feel like minus ten. We were wimps!"

"You are laughing now, but do you remember the tears when we first moved up here? Remember, how intimidating the land was?"

"Uhm," I sobered up a bit as I remembered our first trip up to the property after the snow melted. We had purchased the house, after that one trip up before Christmas. We had never seen what it looked like at any other time.

We came up from Toronto for a long weekend. We were both anxious and excited. Renovations were underway. We had decided to fix the house up and build an extension. Instead of staying at a motel in Sturgeon Falls, we purchased an air bed and decided we would camp out in the construction zone.

Everywhere we looked we saw trees. There were no signs of the river. The forest around the clearing, where the house stood, was as thick as can be. We tried to take a walk and found ourselves fighting underbrush, mosquitoes and darkness. I know we were shocked at the overgrown and poorly maintained state of the land surrounding the house.

Ric broke the silence by saying "I was so intimidated after that first trip up."

"I know – everything looked completely different. Nothing like what I had imagined. I had visions of blue water, rolling green hills and..."

"Instead we had an unruly, overgrown forest – acres of it," Ric interrupted. "Remember how you used to ask me how big is an acre?"

"Yes, I used to ask you to put it in perspective, by comparing my walk from the condominium to the bank on Bloor Street." I said with a chuckle.

"We probably could fit the whole block around our Toronto building into just a small portion of our property," Ric exclaimed.

"Sometimes I feel like this is a dream and I am going to wake up in Toronto," I whispered.

Ric's face softened as he too went into a contemplative mode. We both find it hard to believe that we are here. Life has been a journey, almost an adventure, with many ups and downs. I often look back and know that I would not change anything. It is possible that a different choice would have changed the present completely. What if I had never left India? What if I had not gone to Africa or not come to Canada? My life would have taken a different path altogether.

Unexpectedly, my eyes filled up and tears warmed my face. I felt overwhelmed with emotions. The what 'if's' of the past caught up with me.

"Why are you crying?"

"I am happy, these are tears of joy. Every day that we are alive we make choices and each choice that we make could lead us down another road. I am happy that we made the choices we have to be here."

"Kashmir Acres?" Ric asked.

"That and us, everything – all of it!" I said. "Was it not the very first year you named it –Kashmir Acres?"

"Hmm ... yes, I think so. The mountainous terrain, majestic evergreens, a river as wide as a lake – they all reminded me of your descriptions of your birthplace – Kashmir."

"It is the perfect name. I love the sound – cash-meer" I let it roll off my tongue. It has a decadent, silky and luxurious sound.

"Ten years ago, the work that needed to be done to return this land to its former glory, felt like a mammoth task – a huge elephant hanging around our necks. It was intimidating. I used to feel this sense of urgency and inadequacy – almost fear," he recalled.

"We have come a long way, my love," I commented with a bright smile. "Now, I am hungry. What's for lunch and did you think about dinner?"

"You and your dog are always hungry," Ric grumbled, as he went to get some lunch ready for us.

Sleepily, I looked at the fire – I am very pampered. Ric does look after me. It has been a great partnership, I thought. Starting a business together, getting married, moving north and learning new things. I remember how daunting the whole country-living idea felt, once we saw the land. I pictured lazy days, laying in the sun by the river and trying my hand at fishing. I dreamt about kayaking along the shores of our property. Relaxed walks as we enjoyed nature and the quiet rural atmosphere.

That first year, we came up in the early summer, to enjoy a few days off work. We could not find our way to the river. We knew it was close by but the thick forest and undergrowth seem to prevent us from finding it. Ric decided to go into the Canadian Tire in Sturgeon Falls to purchase a brush cutter and a few other supplies. Ric taught me how to use the brush cutter and both of us went after the underbrush with a vengeance. Ric began by clearing the area around the house and I took off in the direction that we had walked in the winter, before we purchased the property. I was determined to win the battle of the overgrown weeds and clear a path to the river. I had to come back to the house a few times to refuel both the machine and I. A few hours into this activity and I began to feel like I was cutting down giant trees. My muscles ached and I was hot. I was thinking about taking a break when the brush cutter shut down. Decision made, I thought and headed back to the house.

Ric could not get the machine going. It was only a day old, so he decided to head into Sturgeon Falls and see what the store could do to fix it. As it turns out, they just replaced it with a new one. They figured it must be defective, since it had been used only for a few hours.

"Lunch is ready, would you like to eat at the fireplace or go into the sunroom?" Ric's voice brought me back to the present day.

"Do you remember that first summer, when we came up from Toronto?"

"Which time, we drove up a few times? Ric asked.

"Oh! I was thinking about the one where I tried clearing the path and broke the machine," I recalled with a laugh.

"What was funny about that episode were your trembling arms and quivering legs. As I recall, you could barely move that evening." Ric said with a smirk.

"That seemed to be the theme that year. I had aches where I did not know muscles existed. It was exhilarating, though. Don't you think?" I asked, grinning.

"It sure was." Ric observed. "Aching muscles, tired bones, dirt under our nails and on our skin, nothing could faze us. We were loving every bit of the adventure. Though I have to admit, I felt like we would never get anything done. The property was huge in my eyes. It seemed like an uphill climb, with the summit moving further and further away."

"The gym never prepared us for the workout we got outdoors that's for sure."

Smiling as he recalled that morning, Ric exclaimed, "Remember that time, we woke up and the air mattress had almost deflated!"

I burst out laughing as the memories came flooding back. The house was a construction zone and even though we had cleaned the floors, we missed a nail. It did its trick and by morning our brand new air mattress had a tiny hole. I came up with some theory about placing it in water and the bubbles would help us isolate the hole. Once we knew where it was we could fix it. Typical me – the mattress was a king size one – not sure where I thought we could submerge it.

"What I enjoyed most of all were all the delicious meals." Ric said softly. "Winning that barbecue was a stroke of luck. We never thought we would be able to use it."

"It was the Princess Margaret Lottery, was it not?"

"Yes, it was."

"What did we do with it? I don't remember storing it in our tiny condominium locker. Was it at the office?"

"No, I stashed at my parents' home in Fonthill."

That first year was such fun. Ric's parents loaned us their cooler and we purchased one. Before we came north for the weekend, we would go shopping at Kensington Market. I would marinate chicken, pork, lamb or steak in containers. We'd buy fresh vegetables, eggs and bread. The menus were planned in Toronto. I would write everything down, pack spices accordingly and Ric would pack the coolers with all the food and ice. We had a few cast iron pans that we'd bring up with us.

The construction crew used to tell us that the food smells at breakfast and lunch were sheer torture. Ric would serve toasted bread, fried eggs, bacon and home fries for breakfast – all done on the barbecue. There were no appliances in the house – in fact there were sections totally open to the outdoors. All the meals were prepared outside – it was a very special time.

Without fail, on the day that we had to leave for Toronto, my eyes would fill up with tears. I did not want to go back. Ric found it harder and harder to get going. We would delay our departure time or we'd call the office to make sure all was well and extend our stay by a day.

"Remember that large storage chest we found by the old garage – it was used to store some fishing supplies?" Ric asked.

"Oh! I do – we scrubbed it clean and used it to store all our brand new china and pots and pans." I remember feeling extremely resourceful and innovative. After all, it was a dirty old outdoor chest used for storing fishing supplies, pails and an old anchor.

"Yup! I purchased a lock and we left behind all the stuff you were buying on the Shopping Channel for our second home." Ric said.

Once in Toronto, I did not feel all that clever. "I remember checking the weather and it showed snow up in Field and I was scared the plates would freeze and break."

Ric reached over and placed his hand on my wrist, as we got lost in memories again. I had never thought about frost or frozen ground. We put in an offer on the house in December that year. It was accepted just after Christmas with a closing date of January 31. We were anxious to start renovations and construction, but the contractor told us that the work could not begin as the ground was frozen.

For the first time in my life, 'snow' meant more than just something the happened in the winter. We needed to have the septic tank inspected. I had been speaking to the person, in North Bay, who would send the inspector to our home. It was April and they said they could not do so as there was too much snow. I had to read up on septic tanks – certainly living the urban life, I had not given wells, septic tanks or sump pumps any thought.

"You know," Ric's deep voice broke into my thoughts, "I could not have done this without you. I always dreamt about owning my own business and I knew I needed the right partner to make it happen. Without you I could not have done it."

"Without 'us' it could not have happened. It took both of us to get here. It took both of us, together, to get out of the financial mess and difficult times. I think without the balance we created together, none of this would have been possible." I said with great passion. I really truly believe in my heart that we have been equal partners. I am his 'yin' and he is my 'yang' - two parts that create one whole.

Just as the sun rises to create light and it sets to provide darkness, I believe life is all about opposing forces creating complimentary rhythms. Parings like: despair-hope, sadness-happiness, courage-fear, love-hate, anger-empathy and so on. I am not sure that life can ever be smooth sailing – there are changing winds and tides.

We are who we are because of each other. We are where we are because of the choices we made together, as a team. We accepted accountability for our actions. When we failed, we took blame collectively and when we succeeded we accepted the credit. In my heart, I have always known that it is not an individual thing – I found contentment, after I met Ric. Neither of us is perfect. Actually, we both have more flaws than there are bees in a hive.

We both have no other close relationships – neither family nor friends. I tend to have many introspective moments and during those quiet times, I question the idea of human connections. How is it that one is instinctively drawn to some people, while shying away from others? Is it a chemistry thing or is it even deeper? Obviously, we are very complex beings. Over the years, I have started to believe that our subconscious defines our external relationships.

When I think about my inner voice or my internal relationships – the essence of who I am, I realize that those create the external bonds. The things that irritate me about others, can be things that bother me about myself. The key has been to accept the subjectivity surrounding relationships and the changing nature of what we seek in each other. As we age together, there have been countless times, where I think about asking Ric to do something and he has just done it. Times when I think of a simple thing, like 'chicken for dinner' and he brings some in from the freezer.

As my internal dialogue finds peace with those inner conflicts, my external relationship with Ric finds growth and change. I believe...

"Remember the time we took a walk in the woods, that first summer," Ric said with a chuckle,

Drawn back to the present, I said "The time we were introduced to the reality of country living – bugs!" I exclaimed.

"By the time we got back to Toronto we had itchy calves, just above the sock line."

"We could not believe anything could have found their way past thick jeans and socks." It did not take us long to figure out why the locals tucked the bottom of their pant legs into the socks. During the black fly season, there is no choice. These tiny little bugs pack the worst bite ever. They are even worse than the large deer flies – at least we can see and hear those coming.

"Oh! I had welts and swollen red sections that itched even worse than a mosquito bite."

"You are definitely allergic to bug bites because mine do not swell up like yours," Ric remarked.

"I will never forget the moment when I walked into the Shopper's Drug Mart, just south of us on Yonge Street, to purchase something for the bites," I told Ric with a laugh. "I have no idea what I was thinking about. I began by asking the pharmacist for help with the bites. She suggested we try an ointment that contained hydrocortisone and as we walked over to the aisle, I started blabbing about our trip north. I really was acting like a kid who had just opened their Christmas present." I said

"We were pretty excited," Ric replied.

"It gets worse. I don't think I ever told you this part. Not only did the poor lady think I was a bit crazy, she was trying her best to get away from me, gracefully. We found the ointment and she thought she had made her escape – only I followed her." As the memory came back, I just laughed harder. She had looked at me as if I had lost my mind when I pulled my pant legs up to my knees and with great pride asked her to look at the size of the bites I had acquired 'up north.'

GARDEN UP NORTH

As we stopped laughing at my giddy excitement and foolishness at the store, we found ourselves talking about our early experiences. It did not take much for me to lose myself in the past and the start of a new chapter in our lives. I actually remember it like it happened an hour ago – digging our first garden. I remember every achy, sweaty minute of the first day that went into creating our first vegetable patch.

I had read in one of our gardening books that the best spot is sheltered from the wind and gets lots of direct sun. Much to the amusement of our family and friends we used to buy beautiful books on gardening - even though we did not have an inch of outdoor space. Ric loves to quote Walt Disney. He reminds me all the time, "If you can dream it, you can do it." Well, we purchased books and dreamt about gardens.

At Kashmir Acres, the second summer after we had purchased the property, we picked out a section by the new garage on the south west side. This little patch of grass and weed was going to be our first vegetable garden. The section had rich, deep green grass and pretty yellow flowers. I took this as a good omen – the soil must be rich, if the grass is so healthy. The pretty yellow flowers belonged to a weed called dandelion, which later on in our gardening life became a real pain to eradicate.

Ric purchased two shovels, one wheelbarrow and we set off to create our patch. The trick, as he told me, was to cut out small sections of the sod, shake off some of the soil and place the sod in the wheel barrow. We planned to dig up a thirty-foot by thirty-six foot plot.

It was a glorious day, bright sunshine, warm breeze and the sound of birds singing. Missing from our space were traffic sounds or fumes. No sirens, no screech of brakes or the blare of horns.

Ric placed the shovel in the ground and gave it a push in with his foot, breaking the sod. He continued the same, until he had a two foot by one foot section. Following his technique, I joined in.

"Nothing is happening," I lamented, pushing the shovel into the ground and trying the foot technique.

"Put more muscle into it," Ric advised.

I used all my strength to try and break ground. Finally, I felt the sod give a bit. I pushed harder and got a bit of a break in the sod. I looked over at Ric, he was drenched, the sweat was just pouring off him like a little river.

Eventually, I had a small square of sod separated. By then Ric had more than ten feet dug. I never expected the soil to be so hard. When we visited my in-laws, the soil in her flower beds always looked soft and dark. All I glimpsed under the sod was something orange.

"Honey, what am I doing wrong? I can't get this shovel into the ground. Look, I got the tip in and I am standing on it and it is going nowhere." I cried in frustration.

"The ground is hard and compacted, that's all. Why don't you work on separating the sod and getting it into the wheelbarrow?"

I figured I might as well try something else, after all how hard can that be? I knelt down and carefully pried the cut off sod from the soil below.

"Yikes, holy mackerel," I screamed jumping up.

"What's wrong now?"

"There are all kinds of monstrous beings under here!"

"No kidding – you are digging up earth, what did you think you would find?" Ric said exasperatedly.

I decided not to respond – he sounded pretty snotty. Fortunately we had purchased a pair of gloves for me and I did not come in contact with all the creepy crawlies. I was surprised to see little shiny bugs and weird orange snake-like creatures. How do these things breathe in this dense earth. Now earthworms I know about because we studied and dissected them when I was in high school – they breathe through their skin. There was this horrible thick white worm with reddish claws – too ugly for even its mother to love.

"Are you planning on getting anything into the wheelbarrow?" Ric yelled.

Quickly, I grabbed the sod and shook off some of the soil and bugs. It was a lot heavier than I expected. It took some effort to get it into the wheelbarrow. I moved on to the next piece and tried to get myself into a rhythm – lift, shake, toss, lift shake, toss – Sam Cooke's song 'Chain Gang' made its way to my lips. Before long, we were singing away in the sun.

"This beats our trips to the Sky Dome in Toronto," I said. "No crowds, here. I did not think we could find such absolute quiet – a far cry from the constant drone of city noises."

We continued to work, humming quietly. One of the first things we noticed was the clear, pure blue colour of the sky. There is no smog to prevent the real shades from showing – bright, clean blue with a depth that is hard to describe. The breeze helped cool our hard working muscles and the sun warmed my aching back.

"I think we should take a break – I will be back with some water." I told Ric, heading back to the house. I have never tasted anything as fresh as the water from our well. It is ice cold and has a magical ability to quench my thirst. After filling a couple of bottles with water I headed out to sit in the shade and rest for a bit.

"I am having a hard time lifting the sod – it is really heavy." I told Ric.

"Maybe I should cut it into smaller pieces?"

"Hmmmm! This is nice."

"Come on lazy bones, we better get going." Ric reminded me, as he got going from our all too short break.

"Hooh! Aah! Hooh! Aah! That's the sound of us working on the sod," I sang, trying to mimic the beat of Sam Cooke's song.

"Keep you day job!" Ric sang back.

Despite having lived at Kashmir Acres for almost a year, we had not lost our 'city edginess' or the 'go-go' mentality. Once we get started on something, both of us have a hard time stopping. We are driven to complete things.

We'd met Bob and Jacques soon after we purchased the property. They built our garage and helped fix a few things. Bob used to tell us to pace ourselves. "It will be there tomorrow," he'd say. To this day we have to remind ourselves to stop – it will be there tomorrow.

Bob owns a huge property in Sturgeon Falls. He also grew large quantities of vegetables. He began sharing bits of gardening wisdom with me, as soon as he saw us trying to dig up a plot. Sometimes, the easiest way to learn new things is when someone shows you. I love reading and I spend a lot of time researching. But the best lessons came from people in our community. Neighbours who willingly shared their knowledge and experiences in growing vegetables.

In Southern Ontario, people look forward to the long weekend in May – Victoria Day – to start planting outdoors. In Field, everyone warned me not plant outside until June 13, as it is not uncommon to have a really cold spell and frost. "Frost" was another word and concept that completely baffled me. I knew the word, of course, but more in the context of human behavior or frosted nail polish or lipstick. The first summer that we planted a vegetable garden, I did read up on this thing that everyone was afraid of – frost.

I had read that frost forms on the surface of the plants and can damage them beyond hope. One type of frost occurs when a cold front moves in and the other type occurs when the skies are clear and the wind is calm. Radiant heat rises from the earth to the upper layers of the atmosphere. The lack of wind prevents the warm and cold air from mixing. As night approaches, the cold air gets trapped under the warm air and we end up with frost on our plants.

All this sounds great when you read it, but it is hard to believe when the days are warm and the sun shines, daily. In my naïve, I-know-it-all attitude, I went ahead and planted some cucumber plants in May. Frost is a benign concept until one has experienced its attack. Sounds harmless — frost — just a thin layer of ice on the surface — actually very pretty white stuff. I learned the hard way that it is best to listen to others when you have no experience or knowledge in the matter.

Ric had purchased a few cucumber plants for me from a farmer in Sturgeon Falls. They were growing well and were a couple of feet tall by the start of June. I was pretty proud of my efforts until that fateful night and my discovery in the morning. Frost had struck and my plants were dead. Later on I learned that if frost is expected, it is a good idea to drench the ground around the plants with water. Moist soil holds heat better. Light plastic sheets or old blankets can be thrown over the plants for protection.

I knew I had slowed down considerably, as my tiring body brought me back from thinking about frost to the task at hand. My arms ached and my back was sore. The sod seemed to get heavier and heavier as the day went along. I could feel the sting of salt in my eyes as the sweat just poured off my forehead. Time to take a break I thought, looking over at Ric. With a satisfied grin I thought, he too is slowing down. We are going to be two very tired puppies tonight.

Before I could say anything, the silence was shattered by the loud cawing of two crows just above us. I swear the crows up here are on steroids – I have never seen any this big. They have a huge wing span and mimic sounds like a baby crying or a dog barking. They are aggressive, mean and not lovable at all. Though, one year a couple of crows ended up with a little family by our bedroom window. The babies made the sweetest sounds when the parent came back to the nest.

We both were very surprised at how attentive they were of the baby crows. One of them always stayed close, keeping an eye out for predators. In the weeks that followed, we were able to distinguish the sounds this couple made compared to the other crows in our area.

They seemed to have a special tone for each other. The little ones could 'cawwwww' for long stretches when the parents were away. I found the sound to be plaintive, melancholic and sad. If one was a dreamer, which I am, one would think they missed their parents.

Human imagination is a powerful instrument. I believe that the mind has the power to take a thought and make it real. Over the years, there have been identifiable moments, where a dream or a nebulous thought has become our reality. I think creative visualization has a lot of merit. I also know that in our lives we have proved to each other that dreams can come true.

When we hit rock bottom in our careers and saw financial ruin, there is no way we would have believed that in less than twelve years we could own a successful business, a condominium in downtown Toronto and the property in Field. Nevertheless, we never stopped dreaming and visualizing.

Inner darkness is a very dangerous place. Self-doubt can become debilitating. It cripples the mind and the body. It buries the instinct for survival. It is a thick fog that is hard to shake off. Once it gets its claws into the inner psyche, it is hard to dislodge. In our moments of darkness, we worked hard at creating positive energy and visualizing good things. Money is not an essential ingredient in the recipe for positive thinking – we proved that over and over again. However, in order to fight the threatening fogs, we had to commit to the positive, either by writing it down or in our case saying it aloud.

We understood the power of our minds in creating success. At the core was our commitment to positive thinking. I am not sure why, but it seems to me that it is easier to wallow in negative energy than to create positive actions. Each of us has the power within to harness the energies that surround us. Yet the pressures of life, the daily grind, prevents us from realizing our full potential.

A word that we used a lot, once we moved to Northern Ontario was "daunting." Acres and acres of land choking with weeds, underbrush, fallen trees and young saplings trying to reach to the sun. On the riverside of the house, the forest was so dense that the sun could not break through. We could not see even an inch of the river, though it was not that far away. In fact, one day Ric took his brush cutter and started cutting a path in the dense growth. He discovered a swing set that was completely invisible from the clearing. He found a couple of rusted old bicycles, an old stove and plenty of tires. Most days when he was headed out to work on the land, he could be heard muttering to himself, "Another daunting task ahead of me!"

"Cawww! Caw, caw, caw," the loud cries of the crows shattered the quiet.

"Yah, yah, yah!" I yelled back at them. "Go away. Find another spot."

"Time to take a break?" I asked.

"You go on in; I think it is time to call it quits for today. I am almost done digging, we can work on the sod together, tomorrow," Ric replied, as he stretched his back, with a grimace. "I think we are going to be sore tomorrow."

"Oh! I am sore now. My glutes are crying big time." I retorted, trying to straighten my back.

With a groan and the help of the wheelbarrow, I managed to standup. My knees were sore from kneeling in the grass. It felt really good, all this hard labour. I felt a surge of joy as I looked at the exposed soil – no sod hiding the lovely hard orange soil where I would plant my vegetables. Slowly I turned to look at what Ric had accomplished – I know he had done most of the work. I could hear him muttering every now and then "This sod-busting is a daunting task."

"What the devil!" I exclaimed to myself, as I looked at our handiwork. "Honey, I thought we were creating a rectangular patch, were we not?"

"Yes, sweetheart, that is what we are doing." Ric said, sounding tired and irritable.

"Stop! Take a look – see what I mean?" I shouted out.

Ric shook his head as he stepped back to look at his handiwork. The rectangle had become a triangle. As the day progressed and the muscles ached, Ric had created a three sided garden patch, instead of a four-sided one.

"Damn! Next time I will use pegs and mark out the section – no more eyeballing." He said as he burst out laughing. I could not help but join in the laughter. A triangle is better than no garden at all. I figured we could fix it next year.

Tired, sweaty, hungry and happy we headed in for the day.

Gardening Lessons Learned—Crops in Pots

Containers have provided us an opportunity to enjoy small scale gardening both in the winter and during the season. Tiny 2 gallon fabric pots are perfect for leaf lettuce and herbs. Ten gallon ones provide us with new potatoes very early in the season. Patio style tomatoes and cucumbers work well in large pots – we add spinach, Swiss chard, collard and mustard greens in the same pots. Greenhouse containers provide us with eggplants, okra, peanuts, green onions, hot and sweet peppers to name a few.

Introspections

It is not unusual for me to tune out of the present moment – in a daydreaming sort of way. Sometimes it can be for just a few minutes and at other times much longer. It is a mental state where things are not in focus – there are only muted sounds, hazy images and my inner-self drifts without purpose. I am sure Ric will suggest this is due to my advancing age – two years past the grand old age of fifty!

As far back as I can remember, people were always yelling at me. The words, whether in Hindi, Punjabi, English or Kiswahili, always translated to, "Where are you?" Needless to say, I did not respond back with, "Bonding with my inner-self!" Usually I would return to the present feeling somewhat guilty.

I enjoy silence a lot. When I was a young teenager, I would climb up to the roof and just hangout. In Africa, I recall many moments at a place called Fig Tree Camp, where I would stare out at the Mara River lost in my own world. As I age, I do not think these times of contemplation have increased but I am beginning to understand what makes me withdraw. Sounds sap my energy and tire me. This is my body's way of coping.

In Toronto, I developed a problem with vertigo. As part of the situational analysis the specialist sent me to Sunnybrook Hospital for a hearing test. My hearing was classified as 'supersonic' – I could hear sounds that the average human could not. Today, years later, I wonder if this is why I have a low tolerance for noise and need to soothe my inner-self so often. Or is it simply my selfish-self, indulging in rituals?

There are times when I focus back with new ideas or remember things from the past that are relevant now. The year Ric and I met always stands out - the excitement of falling in love. The rush of emotion, the heady pleasure of being together and the feeling of well-being. I had to travel to Costa Rica for work. To this day, I remember calling him from Miami Airport, collect, just to hear his voice. It was well before the time of cell phones.

I was working in the travel business and was in Costa Rica setting up tours. We were looking into lesser travelled, more remote routes that would attract the adventurous Canadian. I remember seeing a payphone as we drove towards the rain forest. The poor driver was shocked at my screams to stop the vehicle and reverse back. I stood in the pouring rain and called Ric, collect, again. Ric's phone bill was huge that month.

Some things mellow with age and love seems to be the same. Then, I described my feelings as being thrilling or intoxicating or exhilarating or breathtaking. Today those feelings translate into words like contentment, completeness, well-being, serenity and happiness. We can still get ourselves into a good fight, though not as often as when we were younger.

There are moments when I think about the 'life choices' we make. Can the selection change 'life's path? For example, the day we called our real estate agent and told her we were not interested in going north of Toronto. Within hours we had reversed the decision and decided to come up and check it out. Was that moment, that choice pre-destined? Both my grandmothers believed in destiny. They were certain that there was a map set out for our lives from birth to death. They understood the concept of rebirth, life after death, and the reincarnation of souls. They did not see death as an end, just as a beginning. Choices made in this life would impact the next one. I would listen to them and just took their words in my stride – I did not believe nor did I not believe, if that makes sense.

There are moments in our lives, since that time in India, where I take pause, I stop and reflect. Like the time in Nairobi, Kenya, when an Indian priest who we had never met before, who did not speak English, told me to tell Ric that he believes that their paths had crossed in another life. He then told me about a time when Ric had almost drowned and still carries the scar on his forehead. "Bet you are making this up!" I thought, since I knew of no such incident nor did I recall seeing a scar. As it turned out the scar was hidden by the hairline and the event was true – it happened when Ric was sixteen.

Soon after we found the property in Field, we were visiting my in-laws for Christmas. I was sure they would be upset with us for considering something so far away. Over the last decade we had become close. Ric's dad, Al, surprised us both by encouraging us to pursue our dream. His mother, Ruth told us, "We will probably have longer visits and more quality time together, if you move that far north."

Scared, but excited, we did put in an offer for the property – it was accepted quickly and the two urbanites were headed north. We knew it was a big and very different step for us. We knew nothing about living in a house or in the country. Urban apartment or condominium lifestyles don't have much in common with rural living.

Were we destined to find Kashmir Acres? Was learning to enjoy gardening part of some great cosmic plan? I have no answers, but I am glad we made it north to Field.

Gardening Lessons Learned—Raised Beds

Our outdoor raised beds have been the perfect way to lengthen the short growing season found in a cold northern climate. These structures vary in height from eight inches to 24 inches. Ours are just under three feet wide and over 20 feet long. The soil warms up very fast in the spring and it drains well. Weeding is a breeze and we plant flowers in with the vegetables and herbs to attract pollinators like bees.

Black Gold

"Here, you get that end and we can shake the soil off together," Ric guided us. As the day progressed the pieces of sod seemed to get heavier. We were almost done – our first vegetable almost triangular patch was minutes away from being created.

"Ric, do you remember what the construction crew told us, last year?"

"About what?"

"They said nothing grows up here – there is only clay, no soil. They said we would be lucky if we can grow potatoes." I lamented.

"All the more reason for us to succeed. You wanted a garden you are going to have one," Ric said with great conviction.

"I read up on 'clay' in the gardening books. It is a type of soil– orange and dense, just like what we uncovered. I never really gave 'soil' much thought – soil is soil, but now I realize there are different kinds."

As I read through several books, I had a sense of déjà vu — I think we had studied soil structure in high school. Clay, silt, sand, limestone, loam and peat are all types of soil. Clay is very heavy and hard, when it is dry. Ours was hard like a brick and very difficult to dig. At the lowest points of our property, closest to the water, we have sandy soil. In contrast to clay, it is white and very light.

Along the shallow sections of the river, under water, we have silt. It is slippery and greyish in colour. If we could combine the three types of soil clay, sand and silt, we would have the perfect gardening mix called loam. Clay soils hold moisture for a long time, as I discovered. One time

I dug a hole and filled it with water. It took fifteen minutes to dry out, whereas a hole in the sandy section is dry within minutes.

In those early days, I despaired – the clay soil was winning. I wanted to make it soft and pliable. I figured all I had to do was dig it up and break all the clumps down and I would have soft soil. No such luck – as soon as it touched water, it would be hard as a brick.

Ten years later, I can attest to the fact that clay is a gardener's best friend. With a little work, it is perfect for growing crops. The original triangular patch has the best, most pliable soil of all our gardens.

The first winter we were at Kashmir Acres, we met Yves Rivest. He has a business based in Field – they have a multitude of services, including snow removal. In the winters he'd drive up in a big John Deere tractor-plow machine and clear the snow off our driveway. In the summer he brought in truckloads of gravel for the same driveway. Mr. Rivest has since retired, but his son Marcel continues to help us out.

Once we had removed all the sod, it became clear that we would need some soil. The patch was thirty feet wide, at one end and three feet at the apex. The two sides were 45 feet and 36 feet. It was an odd shape, but I was mighty proud of it. Ric called Mr. Rivest to find out where we could get some soil.

"What did he say?" I asked jumping up and down.

"He assures me they have really nice quality soil," Ric replied.

"So, when can he bring us some?" I asked impatiently.

"Bit unusual for you not to ask how much it is going to cost?" Ric risked saying.

"OK, how much?"

"Far more than you would believe. It is …"

"I don't care what it costs. I want soil, now!" I demanded, interrupting Ric.

"You'd think I was buying you a truck load of diamonds," Ric said with a delighted smile.

Grinning back, I said, "Even better, it is a truck load of dreams! So when is he coming?"

"Not for a while. The rain we had a while back has made the soil too wet. He has to wait for it to dry out before he can load into the truck." Ric informed me.

"Wait, wait, wait – I have to wait for everything. When am I going to start planting," I cried in exasperation.

"Remember, Bob told you not to plant too early." Ric admonished.

With a pout, I took off into the basement to look at my experiment – the seedlings. Ric took me to a gardening trade show of sorts, early in the year. They had a guest speaker who was focusing on starting seeds in the house. We drove to North Bay for the event. It was my first gardening lesson. The speaker had tiny seedlings on a table and he showed us how to transplant them into larger pots. It was fascinating, yet scary. I watched as he handled the delicate seedling. In my heart I knew, I'd break it.

By March of that first gardening year, we had set aside a section beside Ric's workbench in the basement for me. We purchased two fluorescent lights that were twenty four inch wide and were meant for indoor plants. Ric hammered a few nails in the ceiling beams and hung the lights using chains. By the third week of March I had planted seeds for two types of tomato plants – Roma and Beefsteak.

In addition, I planted catnip, French marigold, chives, bush basil and cilantro. Since we had moved our business from Toronto, we had a nice basement office. It was located right next to the unfinished basement section that hosted Ric's workshop and my little seedling spot. In between client calls and telephone interviews, I would check the soil in the tiny cell packs to see if the seeds had sprouted.

To this day I recall the joy, the excitement and the tears when the tomato seeds broke ground. It was my moment of learning ecstasy. On that day I caught the gardening fever that has not left my veins, even after ten years. I felt foolish and giddy as I wept – it was the tiniest green speck, but it was ours.

I am not sure why I wanted to grow Catnip – we have no cats. Somewhere along the line, I purchased a plant or threw some seeds in front of the house – my notes were not very complete. We have one plant that sends off newer plants in all directions. It is invasive and hard to eradicate, much like mint. In the summer it has exquisite purple flowers that the honey bees adore. I have pulled clumps of the original plant and planted them in other parts of the property to keep our hard working bees happy.

As my seedlings grew, I started to read up on things that could go wrong. I had become attached to the tiny plants and feared for their well-being. I had to curb the urge to over water them. I became somewhat obsessive – checking on the plants every few hours. I would report back to Ric when a new leaf appeared or if I felt the plant had grown a bit.

"Did you hear back from Mr. Rivest about the soil?" I demanded.

"Yes, he said he will be here in the next day or so." Ric replied rolling his eyes dramatically.

"Well. When? Tomorrow?" I said close to tears at the casual approach to time.

Patiently Ric answered, "You know this is not Toronto. Things move at their own pace in the country. Chill, the soil will be here when the time is right."

Finally, the much awaited day arrived. The precious soil arrived in a huge truck. We both watched with bated breath as Mr. Rivest backed it to the edge of our patch and raised the back of his truck at a slant. I had envisioned us getting on the truck and shoveling off the soil. Apparently the back of the truck just lifts up and slants back dumping the soil.

We were like kids in a candy store. With great enthusiasm, we tackled the pile of dirt getting the patch ready to plant the waiting seedlings. We evened it out over the patch and picked off any stones we found. Ric was smart enough to have purchased a rake – an instrument I had previously encountered. Early in our courtship, we were visiting my in-laws to be. Ruth, Ric's mother, was busy planting flowers in the beds around the house. I was the muscle behind the operation. Well, I managed to leave the rake in an odd spot, forgot about it and then bare-footed stepped on its pointed fingers. It was not a pretty site and we had enough blood around to emphasize my clumsiness. Needless to say, I am extremely careful around rakes in our garden.

Memories have a way of surfacing unexpectedly–my brain tends to create thought lines that challenge me into making the links between thoughts. As I think back to the time we fussed over our new vegetable patch, I recall a few conversations with my in-law's neighbours in Fonthill. I did not realize that I was receiving one of my first gardening lessons.

In retirement, Janet and Hans, had left a beautiful northern home to move south. One weekend we were visiting from Toronto. The complex where my in-laws lived was nestled in a quiet cul-de-sac. Each unit had a separate front entrance. The back patio was separated from the neighbours by a small privacy wall. The back garden was barrier free and easily accessed by neighbours.

Janet invited me to join her on her side of the garden. She had a lovely patch with flowers and herbs. In fact, I saw my first ruby-throated hummingbird, in Canada, sipping nectar out of the flowers in her garden. She introduced me to 'lovage,' an herb that to this day we enjoy. It has a flavour similar to celery with a hint of lime. It retains its flavour and fragrance even after it is dried for storage. In fact, when we decided to leave Toronto and move north permanently, Janet gave me a huge package that had part of her lovage plant in it. We planted it and dehydrated some of the leaves and stored it in the freezer – it flavoured our soups and stews for three years.

Hans and Janet had a fair size vegetable garden, before they retired. Laughing with joy as memories took her back in time, she told me about the time she planted garlic. Hans was an amateur pilot and often flew over their property. She knew it was him checking up on her as she worked the soil. After one such fly-over in the spring, he came home with pegs and ropes. He told her that the garlic she had planted in rows were crooked and looked really odd from the sky. She told me to make sure I marked my rows before I began planting. "You never know who is looking down at your garden," she told me with a smile. Sadly, Hans passed away, Ric's parents moved to a retirement home and I lost contact with Janet.

While I never mastered the art of marking rows, Ric did. Every year, he goes out and sets up the rows for me – tomatoes, potatoes, onion, garlic, peas, beans, beets, just name it- he is ready to follow the directions. All I have to tell him where and how far apart to mark the rows. Despite his efforts my seeds or plants end up being planted crooked. I start out paying attention to the bright yellow rope, but as I get closer to the end of the sixty foot row, I am too tired to stay focused on straight lines.

One summer I was working in the garden and I could hear a plane approaching. It was obviously flying low for me to hear it. I took a break from the soil and stood up to see it fly by. Memories of Janet and Hans flooded my senses. On an impulse, I waved at the plane as it flew over – the pilot responded by dipping the wings, left, right left. I laughed with joy and shouted my delight so loud, that Ric came charging out of the garage, where he had been working. He was sure I had been attacked.

Bringing me back to the present, Ric interrupted my musings with a loud, "What's next?"

"I have to get the seedling out of this pot and plant it in the hole you dug," I told Ric. "It does not say how to get it out though!" I exclaimed in frustration.

"Well what did my mother do with all the flowers she planted with you?" Ric demanded, as if I was an expert after helping her once.

"I don't' know – I just dug holes and put the seedlings in it. She got them out of the pot," I cried.

"Try squeezing the pot," Ric directed.

"What if it kills the plant!" I yelled in frustration.

"Well squeeze it gently and then try turning it upside down." Ric modulated his tone to soothe me.

Eventually, with a few mishaps we had our first vegetable garden planted. With great pride we watched the plants growing and blossoms forming. I had found a sturdy twig that was about fourteen inches long. I sat it against a ruler and with a permanent marker set up one inch, two inches three inches, etcetera markings. This became my favourite tool. In the winter leading up to the first garden, I had researched information on all the vegetables I was going to plant. I had these written on index cards that were filed in plastic sleeves in a photo album.

Before I would plant something, I would go to the appropriate index card and get directions. For example the card for radish plantings said: "Plant seeds half-inch deep, one inch apart. Rows should be twelve inches apart. Thin seedling to two inches apart." The twig ruler helped me measure out distances and depths. Fortunately there were no observers of this attempt at gardening precision and a blatant display of my perfectionist tendencies. In my defense, though, if you have never thought about twelve inches in real time, how would you know what it looks like in the garden? Then again, people that provide growing instructions on seed packets make a lot of assumptions.

We were expecting my family to visit from Southern Ontario that summer. I was very excited about my garden and wanted them to experience firsthand the joys of home grown vegetables. It was still early in the season, but we had lettuce and spinach ready for harvest. We also had really young green onions and the radish plants looked tall enough to be ready for harvest.

When the time came to get dinner to its final stage, with great flourish I stepped outside.

"I will be right back with the salad-fixings!" I sang out to no one in particular.

In no time I had clipped the greens and placed them in my harvest basket. All I had left to do was grab a bunch of radish and I was going to be ready to share our fresh bounty.

I pulled the first radish plant out of the ground and screamed in dismay. I yanked the second plant out and burst out crying. Something was very wrong with my radish "bunches" – there was only one radish on each plant!

Gardening Lessons Learned—Compost

It is such a simple and easy to complete concept. Yet many of us miss out on this valuable garden asset. Within one year of moving to our rural abode, we started composting. Tea bags, coffee grounds, egg shells, vegetable and fruit peels are all converted into a nutrient rich black gold that the plants adore. Our home produces only one full garbage bag every few weeks. Composting and recycling have been two very important steps in reducing our carbon footprint.

ALL CREATURES
GREAT AND SMALL

Once we immersed ourselves in country living, we realized how our behaviours were controlled by invisible influences in the city. In Toronto, we darted about our business – quick steps, economical but fast movements and eyes always looking around, but not at people. We entered elevators and stood erect, looking straight ahead. We walked into the subway or streetcars in silence. We lived in a busy metropolis, essentially alone.

In contrast, in no time at all, we found ourselves slowing down. We no longer rushed from moment to moment. I would go to the library or the post office and what should have been a few minutes could end up being a thirty minute outing. In Sturgeon Falls, we noticed that a simple trip to the grocery store invariably ended up with a visit and an exchange – when the total population of an area is as small as ours, one is bound to meet an acquaintance.

Rural communications and networks beat every hi-tech invention. One year we had some problems with the hot water heater. We decided it was time to replace it. After some research we chose to rent one. As is the case sometimes, the company required us to have some work completed before they would install the heater. Ric called Bob, who referred us to his friend 'Mousie,' who could not help us because his wife was recovering from surgery. However, he asked us to contact, Frank.

Within a matter of hours, we had someone to help us get things ready for the water heater installation. Frank turned out to be a seventy-two year old gentleman with the nicest smile and twinkling eyes. He got a lot of work completed and returned the day the company showed up to finish the job. We would have been lost without his help.

Just two houses south of our property, we discovered a sign on the highway that read "FRESH EGGS." Ric ventured in one day and purchased a dozen fresh eggs – we have been going back ever since. The eggs are delicious and just hours old. As soon as the water heater had been installed, we went into Sturgeon Falls to pick up some groceries. On the way back we stopped in for fresh eggs. Frank was there – he was visiting our egg supplier and his cousin, Gerry!

Over the years we experienced the generosity of strangers and formed many new bonds. We faced many tests, which we would have failed, if we followed our urban training and roots. One of the first incidents happened on a July evening. The day before, we had taken the boat up river, heading north.

The Sturgeon River is flanked on both sides by forests and wilderness. There are just a few houses along our stretch of the river. The river is wide, deep and it has a winding path – so much so that we can drive to the bridge over the river in Field in just a few minutes, but by boat it can take ten times longer.

It was a sunny day, with clear turquoise skies. The wind created a bit of resistance as we journeyed north. Now and then we spotted ducks and mergansers in the reeds. We had been in the boat about twenty minutes when the engine cut out. Ric tried to get the engine started again, but it would not. He had kept a container of gas in the boat and he topped up the tank – still no luck. Finally, we gave up on the engine and started to row downriver.

The currents were strong and kept pulling us in another direction. Soon we came across a large dock on the river. Beside the dock was a clearing and we could hear a four by four approaching the area. Before long, the rider had thrown us a rope and pulled us to the dock. Our rescuer was Heather – after we had introduced ourselves and exchanged pleasantries, we told her about the engine cutting out. It was a brand new boat and motor.

It did not take Heather too long to find the problem. The cap on the engine was blocking an air vent or some such thing. Ric had the engine running again, and with a quick thank you we headed home.

"Another adventure!" Ric said as we tied the boat to our dock and headed up the path.

"I am glad Heather helped us out. I do not think we had the stamina to keep rowing all the way back," I told Ric.

After a hard day outside, we were sitting on our back patio. It overlooks the river and is a perfect spot to enjoy nature. It was early evening and we were chatting. I thought I heard a boat motor coming our way. But it seemed to cut out and then I heard nothing at all. I figured they were fishing in one of the coves around us.

A while later, I heard the sound of a whistle. It seemed to be coming from the river. As it turned out, it was a personal watercraft – the rider was heading down river and ran out of gas. It was our turn to play rescuer. He continued drifting past our house with the current.

"Stay with current!" Ric yelled, "Just past that far curve in the river is our boat – I will get it going and catch up with you."

The rider acknowledged the directions with a wave.

"What are you going to do?" I asked Ric.

"I am going to grab a can of gas and drive down to the boat. It's a good thing I filled all the cans earlier today." Ric remarked as he took off for the garage.

I followed the rider's progress downriver. I could see Ric driving down the path that led to the dock. Before long Ric had the boat close enough to throw a line to the rider and bring him safely to our dock. Once the personal watercraft had been refueled, the rider wanted to reimburse us for the gas.

Refusing to accept money, Ric shared the lessons learned and rural wisdom with him. "Your debt will be repaid the day you help somebody in need!"

Some relationships were fleeting and others continued over the next decade. One stands out as it was a love-hate scenario. We met late June, the first year that our vegetable garden was planted. Ric's mother and I had just finished clearing up the lunch dishes, when Ric came in from outside.

"I just saw something near the vegetable garden. It was brown and it ran off when it saw me."

"What was it? Was it in the vegetable patch?" I yelled as I ran out the door. Ric and his parents followed me out.

"I don't believe this," I cried in disbelief. Where there had been lovely green growth – beautiful leafy lettuce, the broad leaves of bean plants, sweet pea vines – were just a few stumps.

"My beautiful cilantro plants," I hiccupped as the tears flowed. Ric took me in his arms, trying to soothe me.

"We will get this sorted out. We can replant everything," he crooned, trying to console me.

My mother-in-law took me inside and we tried to figure out what had happened. "Rabbits!" she declared. She told me that the rabbits in their neighbourhood ate everything – flowers, herbs, whatever they could find.

Ric and his dad were outdoors for a while. They came in looking grim. The culprit was a 'marmot' or 'groundhog.' They had spotted it returning to the patch and chased it away. Ric drove off to Sturgeon Falls and returned with some chicken wire. While he was gone, I stood at the patch guarding the stumps and crying over my lost plants. We built a fence around the patch to keep the groundhog out.

Over the years, the original groundhog created a family that came to live with us. I researched and tried to find natural solutions to keep them out of our gardens. It became a game, there was laughter at the antics of the groundhogs and then there were tears when they ate my flowers and vegetables.

One year, we woke up to an early morning storm. It was windy and the heavy rain was accompanied by thunder. We were having breakfast on the back patio, when we saw the groundhog emerge from his hole. I guess the rain masked our presence. We watched in amazement, as he effortlessly started to climb up one of the trees, close to the house.

Every now and then, it would stop and dine on tiny leaves and then keep on going up. We watched this for a long time. Ric got the camera and took some pictures of it high up on the tree. Later on we found out that groundhogs swim, burrow and climb. When searching for food or threatened, they are incredibly creative. All summer they gorge themselves on delicacies, like those found in my garden, building up body fat. They retreat into their underground burrows for the winter, returning in the spring.

One summer, Ric decided to investigate the lifestyles of our resident rodents. He was amazed at the ingenuity of these creatures. He found several escape routes, some more than fifty feet apart. In the spring, a few years into our northern adventures, the mother showed up with two babies in tow. She would creep up to the top of our woodpile and look around. Her large dark eyes looking in every direction for danger. Spotting none, she'd scamper back down and return with the little ones. They would play on the wood pile, while she regally sunned herself.

It may have been because the property was overgrown, when we moved in but we had more 'bear encounters' in the early years than later on. A few times we called the Ministry of Natural Resources, because a bear was coming up to the house. We still have the garbage can that the bear tried to open – it has a hole where its sharp claw punctured the hard plastic.

We were both pretty scared of the bears. One day a bear cub showed up at our back deck. Ric scared it off by banging a couple of pots. It climbed one of the large trees beside the house. Eventually it came around to the front lawn and started ambling toward our neighbour's house. Even though the house is far way and we cannot see it, sometimes the sound of the kids playing travels to us on the river breeze. On this day, we could hear the children playing outside. In a panic Ric called the neighbour.

"Hello," the phone was answered on the second ring.

"It's Ric, your neighbour to the north," Ric stated with a bit of urgency. "There is a bear cub headed your way. I think your kids are outside." Ric warned.

"Oh, that cub was on our kitchen's roof yesterday. The kids are well trained and they have whistles and know what to do," she replied matter-of-factly.

Our northern lessons had commenced–we would learn to share the land with all creatures. We would learn to respect their space and their role in our lives.

Gardening Lessons Learned—Vertical Growth

For years we tried to outwit raccoons who would devour our ripe melons in just one night. Slugs would damage our cucumbers as the vines spread through the garden and the fruit lay on the ground. Amazingly these plants are natural climbers. I plant the cucumber seedling or seed beside a trellis. When the first vining tendrils appear, I coax the stems to start climbing the trellis. We have a small greenhouse that the raccoons have not been able to get into – here I plant melons and train the vines to climb up the trellis. The fruit is heavy and needs some support. The melons are slipped into pantyhose, which is tied to the trellis frame.

TIME TRAVELERS

"Clang, clang, clang!" the century old school bell slapped against my thigh, as I worked in the garden. This was our latest 'bear deterrent.' The old brass bell, with its magnificent wooden handle had belonged to Ric's Great Aunt Florence. At the turn of the century, in the 1900's she was a school teacher in Missouri. Her life story is full of mystery and intrigue. Many years ago, Ric's parents travelled to Missouri to connect with this elderly relative. She in turn sent the bell for Ric.

"Why not?" my inner voice said, as I took a break from weeding and sat staring at the river, under the shade of a majestic birch tree. Could Great Aunt Florence have seen this moment in time, I wondered. The bell made its journey to Canada, well before I did. Was it destined to chase away bears at Kashmir Acres?

I was first introduced to Gene Roddenberry's, 'Star Trek' television series in the nineteen eighties, when I moved to Canada. It captured my imagination and became my little dream world of human possibilities. The series validated some of my unspoken beliefs about the power of the human mind.

Sometimes I make connections and see things that seem a bit bizarre, even to me. Yet I cannot help wonder about the universe and its mysteries. After all I grew up reading Hindu mythology, where time travel is mentioned in a book that is hundreds of years old – the ancient 'Mahabharata.'

To this day an old memory stands out – my grandmother and I, sitting beside an ancient well in a courtyard, talking while she applied henna to my palm. She used to tell me that I would travel over the oceans to a land far far away. Can some people see the future or have they been there and back? Or is it human intuition that reads current behaviours and predicts future actions?

A beautiful Gray Jay or Whiskey Jack landed just a few feet away. I watched it peck away at the ground looking for tasty morsels. My mind kept going back and forth in time. Why did Great Aunt Florence send Ric and not his brother or sisters, the school bell – she had never even met him?

The sky was the perfect shade of blue, not a cloud to be seen. It looked cool, crisp and sent out calming waves to earth. Ric's eyes have the same shade of blue, I thought. In the distance, high above, appeared the white plumes of an airplane headed north. The twin white trails cutting a path across the clear blue sky.

Astronaut, Chris Hadfield's version of the David Bowie song 'Space Oddity' popped into my mind. "That's it!" That is all the proof I need. Hundreds of years ago, if we had said that a man would record a song in space or even better that he would sing in harmony with people on earth, we'd probably be burnt at the stake. But it happened. Chris Hadfield recorded a song from space with the Barenaked Ladies lead singer. I know, because I have watched the recording – over and over again.

More than twenty years ago, I would frequent a restaurant, Mei Lin Chinese Cuisine, in Toronto. It was on Yorkville Avenue, close to my apartment. My favourite item was their chicken corn soup with egg drop – it was made exactly like the one my mother used to make for us. The chicken fried rice was exquisite. Their Szechuan dishes were truly spicy and hot.

It was a husband and wife team that owned the place. He cooked and she looked after the front of the house. They both seemed shy and reserved, though they did smile a lot. Often, I would stop at the library and pick up a book to read while I ate alone. One day, it was a quiet lunch-hour, they started a conversation with me. We talked for a while and before long discovered that we were new immigrants. They had come directly from Eastern India, while I had made a pit-stop in Africa. After that day, we always exchanged news and talked about life in general.

The restaurant had lovely green philodendron plants in hanging baskets at all the windows and over the bar area. In Asian countries, this particular plant is supposed to bring good luck and prosperity. My grandmother had one growing in her courtyard – it was huge. It is called the 'money plant' – it is supposed to bring good energy wherever it grows. I happened to be at the restaurant on my twenty-eighth birthday. Just as I was leaving, they handed me a glass with a clipping from one of their baskets and instructions on how to plant it in a pot. The original plant has stayed with us to this day. It has been trimmed back many times and repotted a few times.

Could that have been my first lesson in gardening? It is possible, that some of the early events were part of a bigger picture. Often, I wonder if there are other 'earths' out there – places where another human race carries on the daily grind. Does every action, today, have a connection with the past or the future? Do we have the power to change tomorrow by choices made today?

Janet's loveage plant that had made the journey from the north, to their southern retirement residence and then up to our property, lived only two years. Our resident groundhogs loved it. They ate it that first year, but it did grow back in a few months. However, the rascals ate it again the following spring and the damage was done. The plant never grew back. Eventually, we used up all the dehydrated supplies and that was the end of it.

As our business grew, our lives became extremely hectic. The first person we hired to help us was a friend of ours. I had met Nola, by chance, on my third day in Canada. Through another stroke of luck, I met Ric a few years later. Imagine our surprise when, years later, we discovered that both Nola and Ric were born in the same city and the very same hospital. Even better they are both born under the sign 'Pisces.' Stranger still, all my best friends over time – high school and university, shared the same Zodiac sign.

As the business expanded, Ric invited a former associate and friend to join our company. Irene worked with us for a few years. She and I shared some girly moments, as she taught me how to apply makeup. One spring, Irene and her husband had us over for dinner. In their dining room, beside a large window, was a huge sprawling plant. She told us it was a ficus tree. I was fascinated by its size. Before we left, Irene gave us a small clipping from that plant –which I potted. Eventually, Irene moved on to another position and we continued to maintain a hectic schedule.

As is the case in urban lifestyles, time just flew. On a cold Saturday, we were hurrying through Kensington Market, trying to get all our groceries, when I ran into some friends. They delivered the shocking news that Irene had just passed away – she was barely forty years of age.

Irene's original ficus clipping gift to us is well over eight feet tall. It sits in our main living area and we have a younger tree that I started from a clipping off the original, after we moved north. Many a time, as I walk by the tree, its branches brush my skin and memories of Irene stay alive.

Gardening Lessons Learned—Perennials and Annuals

Perennials are plants that survive our winter and return every spring. Our rhubarb, asparagus, horseradish, mint, thyme, chives, daylilies, wild raspberries and strawberries are all examples. On the other hand, plants that live just the one season are called annuals. In the cold north vegetables like tomatoes, spinach, lettuce and peppers have a short life in the warmer months. Herbs like cilantro, basil, sage and rosemary cannot handle our winters.

OYSTERS ON THE SNOW

"Ladies and gentlemen, as we start our descent, please make sure your seat backs and tray tables are in their full upright position. Please extinguish cigarettes and make sure your seat belt is securely fastened . . ." the voice droned on as the Olympic Airways flight from Athens to Toronto made a stop in Montreal.

The passengers broke into a loud applause as the plane touched-down on the runway. I had flown from Nairobi, Kenya to Athens, Greece on my way to Toronto, Canada. A few days in Athens had not cooled my excitement of breaking away from my roots and travelling to a new land—a rich country that meant freedom and opportunity. As the plane came to a stop, I gazed in wonder at the scene outside.

Everything was white and bright. The doors opened and passengers disembarked. Those of us who were flying to Toronto were not allowed to leave the plane during this brief stop. The air felt cool as it made its way into the plane. In no time I realized that the white stuff was snow.

Whatever happened to spring? I thought to myself as I looked at the icy landscape. I had waited to the very last minute, before my 'Landed Immigrant' status expired to make my entry into Canada. Back home, in Nairobi, people who had travelled to North America had told me to wait until the warm weather arrived in the spring.

"You do not know what a winter looks like in Canada!" they would say, nodding their well-travelled heads at me.

"It is best to arrive in the spring. This will give you time to get used to a new country and a new culture, before you have to deal with your first winter," others would say.

As the cold air fought the temperature controlled interior, I continued to stare outside in disbelief. It was March 22nd - how can there be snow, I thought over and over again. It is supposed to be warm, with flowers blooming. Lost in my thoughts, I realized that the plane had left Montreal. The landscape below was a stark white blanket.

"Nanditta, do you have enough of it?" Ric bellowed into the dark night.

"Almost there – just another scoop," I yelled back, as I turned into the wind and headed for the house.

"That is one cold wind," Ric said with a shudder as he held the flashlight steady on the path just outside the door.

"Brrrr!" I replied as I stepped into the warm house. It was Ric's fifty-eighth birthday.

"It is cold, but worth a quick step outside," I told Ric. "The stars are phenomenal – thousands of tiny bright lights in the sky. What is the temperature?"

With a smile, Ric took the large white porcelain serving dish from my hands and said, "It is a balmy minus 27 Celsius outdoors."

"Remember the dirty mess we called 'snow' in Toronto?" I asked him.

"Yes, I don't think it stayed white for even a minute after it fell – it was usually a shade of beige." Ric said.

"I am not sure it was white when it fell on the ground. I think it was dirty before it hit the ground." I said with a sneer.

"I hated the way it used to melt into dirty brown puddles, making the walk to the office, just nasty," Ric intoned.

"Why did it get so dirty?" I asked.

"Probably pollution, salt, sand and dirt." Ric replied with a shrug. "There are a lot of people and traffic, I am sure all those are contributing factors."

Suddenly, Ric started laughing.

"What's going on?" I asked as my face broke out into a smile. By then he was laughing so hard, he could not speak. Laughter is infectious and I joined in without knowing what was so funny.

"Remember Mel...," Ric hiccuped.

"Gibson?" I cried. "The actor who was rumored to be living in Fonthill?"

Trying to get a hold of himself Ric sputtered, "Mayor Mel Lastman!"

"What about him?" I asked, completely baffled and no longer laughing. My inner voice started to worry – is this what happens when you turn fifty-eight? None of this was making sense. Why is he laughing so hard? I have not thought about Lastman in years – sure the Bad Boy commercials are on television, but…what is going on here?

"He called in the army, during the blizzard of 1999!" Ric finally spat out.

"Well there was a lot of snow," I replied, completely puzzled.

"Look outside, Nanditta, you just came in and there is over four feet of snow on the ground. Mel called in the army for far less than that!" Ric exclaimed.

It all came together and I burst out laughing. Our perspectives have changed so much since then. It was a tough time in Toronto. Everything came to standstill that January. As we continued to reminisce, both of us got lost in memories that went back seven years.

"I had never seen as much snow," I told Ric, "Had you?"

"Well in my younger days we used to get a lot of snow. My grandparents lived in Port Perry and Lake Scugog brought in lots of the white stuff. It feels like the amount of snow in urban areas has seen a steady decline," Ric commented.

"Global warming is to blame," I said nodding wisely.

"There, all done," Ric said, as he carefully placed the last oyster on the fluffy white snow.

"I will take this to the table, while you open the champagne," I remarked, picking up the large bowl. For special occasions, we'd make the trip to North Bay to buy live oysters and calamari. For Ric's birthday dinner, we were serving fresh baked bread, oysters, garden salad and deep fried calamari.

In Toronto, I used to walk over to an exclusive grocery store on Hazleton Lanes – they had a fresh seafood counter with a huge variety. It was expensive and we would pay almost four dollars per oyster. We would buy six and enjoy three each as an appetizer. In North Bay we have been purchasing a box of thirty malpeque oysters for less than fifteen dollars.

A week or so before our special dinner, I combine Vodka and chili flakes in a mason jar. This just marinates on the kitchen counter. A few hours before serving the oysters, I add a dash of lime juice, a few drops of Tabasco sauce, finely minced red onion, tomato and cilantro to the Vodka. A tiny spoon of this drizzled over the shucked oysters in the half-shell is just perfect.

"Happy birthday and I hope this year is even better than the last!" I toasted, while sipping on some champagne.

"Thank you, my love," Ric said with a smile, "This is just lovely. The natural salty juices from the oyster work really well with the Vodka. It packs a punch!"

"I like to mop up the juices with warm bread," I commented.

"Remember how I used to crush ice and put it on the platter for the shucked oysters," Ric said.

"What I remember is the balancing act – the oyster shells tended to slip and you would place some salt to keep them balanced on the ice." I said with a grin.

"Could you have ever imagined that you would just walk out the front door and come back with pure white snow?" Ric asked.

"Never in a million years would I have thought that it was possible – not with the beige snow in Toronto!" I exclaimed as I looked at the beautiful vision of shucked oysters on the half-shell sitting prettily on a bed of virginal white northern snow.

Gardening Lessons Learned—Fertilizers

The first time I purchased a fertilizer, I was mystified at the available varieties and puzzled by numbers like 24-2-8 or alphabets N-P-K displayed on the packaging. 'N' stands for nitrogen and is the first number in the series. Nitrogen helps plant foliage to grow strong. The 'P' stands for phosphorous (phosphate) which develops healthy roots and is the second number in the series. The 'K' is for potassium (potash) which is important in the overall health of the plant. For example, a 24-2-8 fertilizer has 24% nitrogen, 2% available phosphate and 8% soluble potash. Some plants need more nitrogen, others may need more phosphorous – it is important to understand the needs of the plant before purchasing the fertilizer.

FISHING WITHOUT A NET

"Can you believe it is our tenth summer here?" Ric asked, swatting at a fly.

"Technically it is our eleventh," I remarked, trying to change positions, so the sun was not directly on my face.

"I meant, since we broke ties with Toronto, sold the condominium and made the decision to make this our permanent home – not just a summer cottage," Ric exclaimed.

"You are right. That first summer, we were more like guests here. Ouch!" I yelled as the fish scale hit my face. "This is a yucky job," I lamented, trying to get the sticky scale off my face.

"It is a glorious day," I commented, as the river breeze cooled my face. We had been busy all day in the garden and then had headed to our dock to see if we could catch some fish. Some days it is hard to believe that this lifestyle is real – not just a dream or a figment of my imagination.

"Do you remember that first summer we took the boat out to go fishing?" Ric's deep voice interrupted my thoughts.

"I do, I do!" I said with a chuckle. "Was that not the time when we proved to ourselves that we really had a lot to learn?"

"It was fun though," Ric said with a dazzling smile, his blue eyes sparkling.

"Well you are still paying for that mistake, my Old Man and The Sea," I said referring to the famous Ernest Hemmingway book.

"What a catch!" he exclaimed as both of us got lost in memories of that afternoon. We had taken the boat out to a cove, just north of our property. A creek joins the river at this point and fishing is really good.

I have explored the spot in my kayak. It is too narrow at the juncture for a large motorized boat, but it is easy to navigate the entrance by kayak.

Both sides are flanked by tall trees and you can see the old logs that have sunk to the bottom. After a few minutes, it widens into a fair size pond that is about forty feet in diameter. The surface is dotted with water lily plants. At the west end, the passage narrows again and the forest closes in. It is a beautiful spot.

After having looked, with great envy, at the distant views of Lake Ontario from our downtown condominium window, this fishing cove felt like a special piece of paradise. For a while, that warm summer day, we drifted around the area, lazily casting our lines. Now and then, we would spot a duck keeping an eye on our boat. Finally, Ric had steered us close to the 'fishing hole' and dropped anchor.

In those early years, I seemed to fish without catching anything. Ric used to tell me to be patient, "That is why it is called fishing and not catching," he'd say. We had been casting for about twenty minutes and I had to be rescued a few times, as my hook kept getting caught in the reeds.

"I got something!" Ric yelled.

"What, more reeds?" I said with a smirk.

"No, no, Nanditta, this is big!" Ric yelled.

"Oh lord," I cried in fright. I had just spotted this huge whale, beside the boat. It looked like something right out of jaws – I guessed it was a shark. I felt the hair on my arms stand up as I caught sight of the fish, again. It was big.

"What are we going to do?" I demanded.

"I don't know. It is really big. I have to get keep it swimming until it is tired."

"What can I do?" I plead.

"Hold tight—we are not going anywhere for a while," Ric said as the fish stayed on the line. I watched helplessly as Ric held on to the fishing rod and the fish swam beside us. Eventually, Ric decided it was tired enough for him to reel it in. Slowly he managed to get the fish close to the boat. He passed the rod to me and asked me to hang on to it.

He leaned over and managed to grab the fish by getting his fingers hooked on to the gills. Lifting the fish out of the water took some effort, but finally Ric had it flopping around in the boat. It really was a monster fish and it looked mean. I just raised my feet up off the floor and watched it glare at us. It was a nine-pound Northern Pike and it provided us many meals and our first country lesson. We purchased fishing nets! The damage was done though; Ric became a regular at the physiotherapist!

"We are almost done," Ric said, bringing me back to the present day. "I am going to bring the hose over to wash down the deck."

While Ric went to get the hose hooked up, I grabbed the last fish by its tail and began the quick upward movement, tail to head to get the silver scales off its body. The scales are so pretty, almost like mother of pearl – the surface is shiny and the sun creates a spectacular iridescent glow.

"What the Dickens!" I screamed as cold well water hit my back. "Ric stop it!" I yelled, dropping the fish on the cutting board and running away from the water.

"I am going to get even with you for that one," I threatened.

"I was just helping you out – you have fish scales all over you," Ric said with a huge grin.

I continued to scowl at him, as I went about the task of rinsing the fish.

"What do you want to do with the fish guts and stuff?" Ric asked.

"Do you have time to dig a hole?"

"Sure! Do you want it in the rhubarb patch again?" he questioned.

"Yes, that works really well. The rhubarb plants love fish fertilizer and this takes its time breaking down in the soil—sort of a slowly released nutrient-rich treat." I replied, as I headed toward the rhubarb patch before going inside to marinate the fish for dinner.

In Toronto, we enjoyed fresh ingredients from the market. However, nothing compares with the experience of walking over to the garden for dinner ingredients. As I walked by the majestic red-stalked leafy green rhubarb plants, I stopped to thank whatever power that directed us to this beautiful northern paradise.

"Pauline's rhubarb plants are so lucky," I thought to myself, as I remembered that beautiful vegetable was a gift from someone I had met in Sturgeon Falls. We created a brand new patch for the plants, overlooking the river. They have a spectacular view of the water and enjoy sunshine throughout the day.

As we have discovered, life does tend to throw curve balls at us. One minute we are chugging along with a nice plan in place and then something happens – usually beyond our control – and we have to change our course. A few years ago, after a series of unexpected events, we decided that I would seek out part-time employment.

At my new job, I met Pauline. On a cold day during our lunch break, we got talking about pies and desserts. Somehow we ended up talking about rhubarb pies. It had to have been at least seventeen years since we tasted one of our favourite pies. My brother lived in a small town, north of Toronto. Bradford had a really nice country feel to it. Most homes had flower and vegetable gardens. My sister-in-law would use fresh local rhubarb and strawberries to make pies. Ric adored the warm from the oven pies with a dollop of ice cream.

Pauline promised to share some clumps of rhubarb from her garden. In the spring, that year, when the ground was no longer frozen, she invited me to her house in Sturgeon Falls.

"Rhubarb tends to spread and is hard to get rid of it," she told me. "I have been trying to eliminate this patch for a few years, but it keeps coming back every spring. If you miss the smallest root, it will grow back."

"Why do you want to get rid of it?" I asked her.

"We have a lot in the freezer and we are not eating as many pies as we used to. Besides I can get some from other family members" Pauline replied.

With great pride I loaded clumps of roots into the back of our SUV and brought it home. Ric had already been assigned the task of digging up the weeds and sod in a new spot by the old garage, overlooking the river. This was where the groundhogs liked to hangout. I naively believed that the groundhogs would be tempted to eat the lovely green leaves of the rhubarb plant. I had read that the leaves are toxic and can make one sick. I figured they would eat the leaves, get sick and find a new home. No such luck – those guys are born with a sixth sense that alerts them to danger.

Pauline's rhubarb adjusted really well to its new home with us. The plants have spread and in the summer they provide a beautiful resting spot for frogs, ladybugs, worms and snakes. The leaves are large and not only provide welcome shade for small creatures, but also protection from predators. The crisp red stems of the plant are juicy, tangy and delicious.

We met John and Edie a few years back when they moved up from Southern Ontario. They live just a few houses north of us. As is the case in rural lifestyles, everyone looks out for each other without being at the doorstep every day. Ric is not big on socializing – he likes to keep to himself. One day, in the summer, it hit me that more often than not I hear Ric say, "I am just going to take this or that over to John and Edie's."

On this particular occasion, I paid a bit of attention to what he was taking over- it was an armful of rhubarb. We share the abundance with neighbours throughout the summer, so that did not surprise me. What was surprising was his volunteering to take some over, so easily. I should have guessed, but I did not! A few days later, John showed up with a plate of warm rhubarb crumble. Edie makes some amazing desserts and somehow Ric had managed to weasel his way into being at the receiving end of this yummy portion.

"Did you find her?" I heard Ric call out. I came out of my reverie just in time to see our lovely Shih Tzu, Sasha, scampering toward me.

Gardening Lessons Learned—Plant Hardiness Zones

One of the first gardening lessons taught us that plants have different levels of cold weather tolerance. I discovered that North America was divided into hardiness zones defined by the average climatic conditions of the area. The zones help determine which plants will grow in a particular area. This becomes really important when considering plants that must survive the winter: fruits like grapes, apples, berries; flowers, herbs and vegetables. In Canada there are nine zones, the harshest is 0 and the mildest is 8. Take Canada Red Rhubarb variety as an example. It will survive anywhere in Canada, handling whatever temperatures the winter brings. On the other hand many varieties of fruits survive in warmer zones but not our Zone 3.

Sasha – The Prima-donna

I met Ric at J. Canucks, a sports bar, adjacent to the famous Masonic Temple at the corner of Yonge Street and Davenport Road in Toronto. It was a cold, wintery night in February. I worked during the day and went to night school at Ryerson University. It was a ten block walk home, straight up Yonge Street. Once in a while I would drop-in at the bar for a beer and a chat. The owners had become friends and it was a nice interlude in my normally hectic days.

Ric used to take his dog out for one final walk at night and he would stop in at the bar for a night cap, every now and then. The bar had a 'Cheers' feel to it and the owners knew everyone's names. Joe, one of the owners, did not mind Ric sitting at the bar with his lovely Bichon Frisé, Chloe. The female clientele would bee-line to him and the dog. To this day I believe that was his intent – having all the pretty ladies cooing over his dog, while checking him out.

On my thirteenth birthday, my dad came home for a short break from his service with the Indian army. He was stationed in a remote part of the mountains, Ladahk – "land of high passes," bordering Tibet. His gift to me was my very own dog – a Lhasa Apso puppy named Mompy. She was black with a bit of white on her face and was born in Tibet. We grew up together and when my family moved from India to Africa, she went with us. My mother convinced the airline that our dog could not travel in the cargo hold – she actually flew in the aircraft, sitting royally on a seat like any passenger.

Once we were married, Ric and I talked about getting a dog. Our hectic days, busy schedules and condominium lifestyle did not seem conducive to rearing pets. The timing always seemed off. However, that did not stop us from talking about it.

"What kind of puppy would you like to get?" Ric asked one Sunday morning at breakfast.

"I have been partial to smaller breeds. When I was very young we had some large dogs – they were fun, but not really cuddly." I remarked.

"What about a Bichon Frisé?" Ric said.

"Hmmm or a Lhasa Apso?"

"I always thought Apso's were really yappy dogs, like terriers," Ric commented.

"Mine was not bad – she was very aggressive though. She was always chasing animals larger than her. One time she took it into her head to chase a cow off our property. She came back with a broken tooth." I said as memories came flooding back. The horror of the moment, as she would not listen to my cries. She was a stubborn but lovable dog.

"Well, we can start researching kennels for both breeds and then make a decision when the time comes." Ric suggested, "I think we should only deal with a reputable breeder."

"Great thought! It may cost us more, but we will know that the parent dogs are well treated." I replied, nodding in agreement. I reached over and pulled the Classifieds section of the Toronto Star. We made it a point to have a leisurely breakfast on Sunday mornings.

"Here's an advertisement for a Bichon Frisé puppy. Wow! Each one is four hundred dollars," I exclaimed, "I did not think they'd be that expensive."

"Oh! If we go with a reputable breeder, we will likely pay more than that," Ric explained.

Over the years, that followed, we discussed and researched different breeds. Ric was partial toward getting a white dog and I wanted a black one. Somewhere along the line, we started researching the Shih Tzu breed of dogs. The more we found out the more we leaned toward this even-tempered and gentle breed.

Soon after we purchased the property in Field, we started looking for accredited breeders. We found a few just outside the Toronto area. I made some calls to get general information and ask if they would be willing to provide references. One kennel on our list was in Azilda just west of Sudbury—Wenrick Kennels. All aspects of their operation felt good and checked out. I remember everything sounded so distant and foreign to my Toronto ears – Azilda, Sudbury, Sturgeon Falls, Field and North Bay.

Once we made the decision to sell our condominium and move north for good, it was just a matter of logistics. We came up with a plan and started executing it. The primary issues revolved around our business – our staff did not want to move north. We found a way to downsize enough to employ both of us full-time and hire just a few local people. In September of that first year, large moving trucks from Tippet and Richardson, made the journey up the highways to our new location, Kashmir Acres, Field, Ontario.

I have always been scared to handle tiny, delicate living beings – babies, puppies or plants, included. When my niece Tara was born we were at the hospital. When it was our turn to go in and see her I was really excited. However, I had never been in the company of a newborn before. As soon as I saw the tiny little pink bundle, I was paralyzed by fear. In the end I missed out and we have a picture of Ric holding little Tara at the hospital, but none of me.

So it was a big leap for us to adopt a tiny little eight week old puppy. Ric and I had purchased all the things that the kennel had recommended – brushes, combs, bedding, crate, water bottle, toys and of course food!

It was a lovely sunny day, the week before Thanksgiving. Excited and nervous, Ric and I headed west on Highway 17 to Sudbury. It was my first trip and Ric's first in many years. He used to travel to Sudbury for business, well before we met. En route we stopped for lunch and then a little later for final directions to the kennels.

Wenrick kennels is the home of many championship dogs. It is nestled in a country-like setting, with lots of open space. Rick and Wendy, the owners, welcomed us to their home. Even though we had spoken on the telephone and exchanged emails, we had never met. In no time we were surrounded by excited dogs and some shrill barking. Wendy shooed all the dogs away and we headed in the direction of the puppies.

"Your puppy is in that crate along with its siblings," Rick told us, pointing in the direction of a room to our left.

"How will I know which one is ours?" I asked.

"Oh, you will!" Rick exclaimed.

Ric and I made our way into the room, where there was a large metallic crate with four puppies. They were tiny, fluffy and adorable.

We had been warned that they did not have a black or white or a combination of these colours available in this litter. By this time, we really did not care – we were thrilled to be adopting a puppy.

As we looked at the tiny beings, a gold and white ball of fluff climbed over the backs of the others and made her way to the frame. Her tail was wagging and she appeared to be smiling. I crouched down and gently placed my hand on the frame. In seconds, she pushed her way to my fingers and gave them a lick. I was in love, tiny little Sasha came home with us and we added a new dimension to our future northern adventures!

The first thing we understood about raising our puppy was that she had a mind of her own. She did not want to do what we asked and had it in her tiny head that she was going to train both of us to do what she wanted. The battle of the wills began. We had been reading about training and the art of positive reinforcement. The other thing was that young puppies have tiny bladders and need to go out at the oddest times.

That first winter was really cold, or our city blood felt it terribly, with lots of snow. Both of us tried to get Sasha to learn to go out and do her business outside the door. Well her highness would have nothing to do with that – no matter what the temperature, she wanted to go for a little romp in the snow before completing her doggie business.

Before going to bed we would take her out, but invariably she'd wake us up to go out late into the night. This one night the conditions were blizzard like – grumbling under our breath, we both donned on our winter gear and headed out with the pup.

"Come on, good girl, let's go in!" I yelled into the cold night as we tried to get in the front door.

"I cannot get it open," I called out to Ric.

Pushing me aside, he tried the door – it would not budge. We had managed to lock ourselves out of the house and it was just past midnight. The wind chill was horrible as we circled the house, hoping against hope that we may have left one of the back doors open.

"Here, tuck Sasha inside your coat and stand against the back door," Ric instructed as we found a bit of shelter on the back patio.

"What are we going to do?" I cried, "We will freeze to death." I said, holding a now shivering and miserable puppy close to my chest.

"Don't go anywhere, I will think of something," Ric said as he headed to the front of the house.

In the end, Ric smashed the glass on the front door, using a hatchet he found in the garage. Then we had to find something to keep the snow from blowing into the house.

A valuable lesson was learned – since that night, we have always kept a key in a secure place, outside the house. It has been used many times over the years as we somehow manage to lock ourselves out, every now and then.

Valiantly, we kept trying to train Sasha and we felt we were making some headway, when suddenly; she would do her own thing. We decided it was time for some professional interference. We enrolled in 'obedience training' session held in Sturgeon Falls. I was a bit scared as Sasha had not met any other dogs in her young life, since we brought her home from Azilda. I was not sure how she would react. As it turned out, she totally ignored the other dogs, preened for attention in front of the humans and did everything that was asked of her, flawlessly.

"That dog has a split personality," I told Ric after one of the sessions.

"She seems like a different dog when there is an audience," Ric replied.

Sasha's dad or sire was a world champion and her mother or dam was a Canadian champion.

As is the case in the show dog business, no dog born with birth defects can compete. Our little dog had a hernia at birth that disappeared by the time she was twelve weeks old. To this day I am convinced that she sees herself as a cut above everybody – human or animal. When she was a few years old, we were invited by one of our clients, to visit their hotel in Montreal. Our organization had been part of the opening team for the chain's first Canadian five-star luxury hotel, Sofitel, Montreal.

Of course Sasha went with us. At the hotel we were welcomed like V.I.P.'s and once in our room, a cushioned bed was delivered for Sasha. In her welcome basket were doggie treats and bottled water. She just lapped it all up as if this was the treatment she got every day. I was astounded at her behaviour during our stay. She stood upright, ears perked and tail wagging. She never pulled away or tried to visit with guests. In fact, I was asked over and over again if we were in Montreal for a 'dog-show.'

Our room was on one of the higher floors and we had to take the elevator. Sasha, who normally does not like new things, acted as if she had been in and out of elevators all her life. As soon as we'd enter one, she would get out of everyone's way and sit just in front of me. She would keep that position, until it was time to disembark. She'd turn around and look at me, as if waiting for instructions.

For the fun of it I began saying, "OK Sasha, time to get off. Make a left or make a right!" To my utter amazement, she followed the directions. Other guests in the elevator really believed that this was a highly trained show dog. Of course, once we returned to Field, she did her own thing!

Dawn of the North

It was a crisp, clear and cold starry night in November. We had been at Kashmir Acres for one year. Life had a familiar pattern and a new routine that embraced country living. I took Sasha out for a final walk, before we turned in for the night. Ric was going to join me, but the phone rang and he answered it. Sasha and I headed out, after waiting for Ric for a few minutes. His mother had called and knowing them, they could be on the phone a while.

Even though it was late, there was enough natural light from the bright stars that I did not need the flashlight. As we stepped away from the house, I felt a strange presence. The hair on my arms rose as I looked toward the sky. It appeared that our house was trapped within a strange tepee like structure. The apex was just over us. The rest of the structure enveloped us in an eerie, diaphanous shroud. I felt like I was standing inside a large hollowed-out mountain. The silky tendrils shimmered around us. Pale blue-green hues with the slightest hint of pink and violet enveloped my senses.

My heart started to beat real fast and my over-active imagination kicked in. I turned around in slow circles watching these laser like beams move with me. I was sure that there was a spaceship above, with aliens watching us with interest. My mind raced ahead to . . .

"What are you still doing outside?" Ric yelled from the front door.

"Look up" I hollered back.

Within seconds Ric was beside me looking at the sky in wonder. I gripped his arm as if to anchor both of us to our land. I was ready to take on the alien forces, when Ric said, "Wow! Our first Aurora Borealis."

Everything clicked in and I realized that I had been dancing with the spectacular northern lights – a natural phenomenon I had read about, heard about but never witnessed until that moment.

"Wow!" I echoed Ric. We stood hand in hand watching the pulsating ribbons of light until they faded away, leaving us illuminated with starlight.

Ever since we became one with this little piece of paradise we call home, parts of Wordsworth's poem, Daffodils pop in my mind with new meaning:

> *"I gazed—and gazed—but little thought*
> *What wealth the show to me had brought:*
> *For oft, when on my couch I lie*
> *In vacant or in pensive mood,*
> *They flash upon that inward eye*
> *Which is the bliss of solitude;*
> *And then my heart with pleasure fills,*
> *And dances with the daffodils."*

As the years go by our treasure chest of memories overflows. Some soften and fade with time and others are sharp and clear – as if it were the present instead of the past. Sometimes I feel an acute sense of déjà vu, a feeling that I have been in this moment before — if not in this life then in another.

"Is everything OK with your parents?" I asked, as we went back to the house.

"Yeh, she just wanted to touch base – it being Sunday. They are fine, getting mentally prepared for the winter." Ric replied.

"So are we still planning to go down south at Christmas?" I said.

"Yes. Mom and dad are actually excited about coming back with us and spending a few weeks here." Ric said, sounding cheerful at the prospect.

"It will be a nice diversion for them. The winter is so confining as one gets older. Here they will have us around and of course Sasha!" I exclaimed.

We made ourselves comfortable in front of the fireplace, blissfully unaware that we would wake up to a blanket of snow. As has been the case over the years, we both enjoy a few quiet moments in front of the fire throughout the winter. It is a time to reflect and lose ourselves in memories. There have been so many unexpected events, which have connected seemingly unrelated moments in time.

For example, a lady stopped by one year and asked Ric if we would like to be part of the local garden tour. She told him that she was a member of the Near North Garden Club and they noticed that we were doing some unique things in the garden. Later in the day Ric told me about the visit. I am a loner by nature. I have never been really comfortable spending time with or meeting new people. I also felt that we were so new to gardening, that being part of a "garden tour" was a bit presumptuous.

The very same lady, Carole Anne, came by the next year. She made an impression on me – her thin frame had an aura of strength. She reminded me of my friend Nola who lives in Toronto. Carole Anne was clearly passionate about gardening and left with a promise that we would participate in the garden tour that year. Apparently the garden tour was very popular. The organizers liked to include ten or so homes with a variety of gardens featuring, perennial flowers and plants, rock gardens, herbs and vegetables.

That summer my parents were visiting form India and we had a lot going on. The week leading up to the garden tour had been cold and wet. Secretly I was delighted because I believed the tour would be cancelled because of bad weather. Even though we saw volunteers stop by our house that Saturday morning to place some signs on the highway, I was sure no one was going to drive out here because of the heavy rain. There also was a cold wind to make things worse.

Ric was orchestrating breakfast for the four of us – hash browns, bacon, toast and fried eggs. My parents had their plates and he handed me mine. Just as I headed to the dining table, I saw a car turning on to our driveway. On that cold wet summer day I understood that gardeners were a breed of their own.

One after the other, cars pulled in and people got out clothed in rain gear and supporting umbrellas. We walked through the vegetable patch, chatting, asking and answering questions. It was a whole new and extremely pleasant experience, despite nature's contributions. I became a convert and lost some of my 'introvert-tendencies' that day. I felt a lovely sense of belonging and a feeling of camaraderie with like-minded gardening souls. A new chapter in our northern adventures began.

Sometimes we take so much for granted. In my case, as a newbie in the field of growing edibles, I often felt left out in gardening forums and discussions. People who have grown-up with vegetable and flower gardens or have been gardening for a longtime have a language that can baffle newcomers.

"Make sure you weed regularly," I was told. In my head I would think "weed what?" My gardening books have pages and pages devoted to this topic. One of the first lessons was learning to identify a seedling from a weed. It was not easy – I pulled many onion and spinach seedlings thinking they were blades of grass. Every year as my knowledge increased, I started to identify weeds found in our garden patch. To this day, I am amazed at the resemblance between some weeds and certain vegetables. There is a weed that likes to grow in between the pea plants. Its leaves look like those of the peas. I know that it takes nutrients away from the garden and I have to remove them. It is not a job for the faint-hearted. One needs surgical precision to pull this weed while leaving the shallow rooted peas safe. I have shed plenty of tears over mistakenly uprooted pea plants.

When I was a young girl, in India, I was very clear in my insect likes and dislikes. I hated mosquitoes and cockroaches. I loved ladybugs and fireflies. I encountered neither the ones I had an aversion to nor the ones I liked, in Toronto. Fortunately, cockroaches do not exist this far north – they simply cannot survive the winter. Blackflies, deerflies and mosquitoes have their role to play for a period of time in the spring and summer.

The first time we planted rows of potatoes we attracted a large and different ladybug to our garden. I was fascinated by the size, markings and colour. The beetles were a pale yellowish-orange with thick brown stripes. The face and under belly were orange, with brown spots on the face. Ric was pretty sure it was not from the ladybug family. I decided it was time to consult one of our neighbours with farming know-how.

"What you have is the potato beetle!" Gerry told me. He grows vegetables just a few houses south of us. Actually, he grows a lot of potatoes to sell throughout the summer. "These beetles will eat up all the green foliage on your potato plants."

"What can I do?" I asked him.

"Well I can give you this white powder that will take care of them. Just dust it all over the plants." As is the case in small communities, he would not take any money for the powder.

A decade later, we still have this pest show up in our garden. Also known as the Colorado potato beetle, it was discovered in 1824 but it origin is unclear. Within twenty years it became the most threatening pest to the well-being of the potato crop. This tiny but mighty beetle, generation after generation, has the ability to build resistance to pesticides. It has been impossible to eradicate these beetles. They have a voracious appetite for the leaves of plants like potatoes and eggplants. The females can lay eight hundred eggs. I have found clusters of orange jelly-like eggs under the leaves. The eggs look like the roe we find in lobsters or fish. Each cluster can have as many as thirty eggs.

One time I was out checking our plants and I came across a cluster of eggs that were just hatching. Tiny reddish-brown larvae were emerging. In no time at all they start feeding on the leaves. Tiny holes start to appear along the edges and as these larvae grow, so does their appetite. In hours they can eat all the leaves on a plant, leaving just bare stems. In about two to three weeks the larvae reach the final stage before they become adult beetles. At this stage they are a pale shade of orange. They fall to the ground, burrow into the soil and eventually emerge as an adult beetle.

Even though we were new to vegetable gardening, in a very short time, we realized the danger in using pesticides. We began to look for alternate ways in effective pest management. I tried spraying garlic water on the little larvae, with no satisfactory results. They multiply fast and grow up too soon. The only method of control that has worked for us is through sheer diligence. The beetles like to feed early in the morning and again late evening. It is possible that the warm sunshine of the day slows them down.

Twice a day during the growing season, Ric and I make our way to the four sixty-foot rows of potatoes, each armed with a pail of soapy water. We hand pick the adult beetles and larvae and drop them into the pail. We inspect the underside of the leaves for masses of orange eggs. If we find any, we wipe them off with a gloved finger. It is hard and messy work but worth every effort – home grown, organic potatoes have a taste and texture that is unrivalled. Growing edibles without chemicals has created a passion and awareness within us. Each of us vowed to reduce our carbon footprint, find ways to protect natural habitats and support local endeavours.

Living this close to nature has taught us valuable lessons—ones that will continue to make us better people and stewards of the land. Cities breed arrogance with invincibility. Nature creates balancing forces that humbles the dauntless. Her power is one to be reckoned with. Nature will not be controlled by the human hand. Moving from the urban centre, Toronto, to this rural spot, Field, proved be our awakening.

Natural Insights

It was a warm sunny day in August. The river sparkled like a diamond necklace. The skies a clear deep blue, the perfect playground for one lone hawk that circled above.

"What are you contemplating?" Ric asked over the happy song of the bees as they buzzed between colourful flowers.

"It has been a decade and what a huge difference this period has made to our perspectives," I replied as a dragonfly tried to land on my chair.

Flicking a fly away from his glass, Ric asked with a puzzled look, "What has?"

"The great Power Outage of northeastern North America!"

"Wow! You have some strange thought patterns," Ric risked. "What took you back to that moment?"

"Sitting here, looking at the river, watching the hawk swoop down, brought home the fact that we have changed so much. That power outage was a big deal, if you recall." I said.

We sat together, in silence, as memories came back in great detail. It was a workday and we had had many hectic weeks. Long hours at the office, quick meals and no rest. That morning we decided to break the pattern by plugging in the slow cooker. We browned the meat, added the trinity – onions, celery, carrots–garlic, red wine and herbs. I came home for lunch and added potatoes and other root vegetables. We were determined to have a quiet and relaxed meal that evening.

With just a few hours left when the last shift ended, we were looking to the next day's schedule. It was just before 4:15 PM–the lights flickered and went out. Immediately, over the muted sounds of the staff interviewing people on the phone, the discordant beeps of the backup batteries could be heard. The east-side wall of the office was glass and light was not an issue. Before long people from other offices were coming to ours asking to use the telephone. Cell phones were not yet mainstream – in fact none of our staff had cell phones. As we all looked out the widows we could see a lot of pedestrians on Yonge Street. There were no trains pulling in and out of the busy Rosedale Subway station. Each visible intersection was a four-way stop and in every direction we saw civilized chaos.

"Remember, how worried we were for John – he lived somewhere in Scarborough." Ric commented as he recalled the huge distance John would have to travel that day without public transportation.

"How did he get home?" I asked, straining to remember.

"I think we gave him money for a taxi, but I cannot remember for sure, what he did," Ric remarked.

"It was such a big deal – we were stressed," I exclaimed.

Ric took a deep breath, as he composed himself. "Well, we were concerned that the clients would not understand the delay in service. I think the backup batteries died sometime that night, as we did not have service the next day."

"In this last decade, we have become stronger and we are not as dependent as we used to be," I remarked, looking at a honeybee disappear into the bowels of a snapdragon flower in search of sweet nectar.

"We were strong in our resolve when we faced bankruptcy, but like many city-dwellers, we were weak when we lost our day-to-day conveniences." Ric commented. "Living in rural Ontario, we have understood human vulnerability and frailty is in essence a result of our sense of invincibility."

"How so?" I questioned.

"In Toronto, we were spoiled and we had it easy. We never thought about running out of hot water or living without electricity. We never gave thought to what happens when a toilet is flushed. We could step out of the building and walk across to any number of stores to pick up anything we needed – cash at the ATM, a hammer or nail, milk or fruit, take-out gourmet meals, just name it and it was right there." Ric observed.

"It made us complacent. So when 50 million people lost power that day across Ontario and in eight American states, it was a big deal. We just did not know how to cope." Ric commented, with a smile. "The isolation of northern communities, like the one we live in, fosters self-sufficiency."

"So true," I agreed. "It has a humbling affect. We have realized the importance of contingency plans and not taking things for granted. Drawing water from a well, having our own septic tank, not having cable television or high-speed Internet are all our daily realities."

"After we moved to Field, we experienced first-hand frequent and sometimes long power outages!" Ric scowled.

"So much so, we have Hydro One's power outage number on speed dial," I said with a laugh. "To this day it never fails to amaze me that we call the outage line and the auto attendant says that there are 363 people in Field without hydro. How do they know?" I wondered.

"Probably it is one grid that serves 363 homes that keeps going down," Ric remarked.

"I just love the incongruity of the questions that the recorded message throws out at us." I told Ric. "Can you see if your neighbour has hydro?" I mimicked the automated recording. "I do not think they get rural living – we cannot see our neighbours – the closest one is far away. Across from us is acres of wilderness and there are no highway lights in our neck of the woods," I cried.

"A valuable lesson, a natural insight was ingrained in us through these frequent outages," Ric said. "We invested in a generator that has been a saviour through many natural disasters, from tornadoes to blizzards."

The word 'tornado' made the hair on my arms stand up, as buried memories tried to break through. Despite the warm August sun, I shivered and tried to block out the brutal images of that fateful storm. Until that ominous evening, I had always enjoyed a good lightning and thunderstorm. My first apartment in Toronto was on the eighteenth floor of the same building that Ric and I purchased our first condominium. It had a southern exposure with a clear view of Toronto's C.N. Tower. On a stormy night, I loved to count the number of times lighting would strike the apex of the tower. The thought of high winds, earthquakes and storms never caused me any concern in those years.

All that changed one July, three years after we moved to Kashmir Acres. We had been plugging away at cleaning the overgrown parts of the property. Our business was busy and we felt that we were not able to devote enough time to outdoor work – we'd clear a section and by the time we finished the next, the first one would need attention again. We had engaged the services of a young man, Shaun, to help us. He would come up from Jocko Point, on the other side of Sturgeon Falls, every Saturday. He loved the outdoors and worked diligently at clearing underbrush and cutting firewood with Ric. They both are the strong silent types and made a great team.

We decided to speed things up by bringing someone else into the mix for a week or so. Through the rural communication systems, Ric was able to engage Ray. Shaun, Ray and Ric went to work to make the property look really good. They removed overgrown saplings and weeds that had grown into large bushes. By thinning out the years of overgrown plants the surviving trees and low growing native plants had a chance of survival. I took the kayak out to observe their work from the river. From the low point on our property I launched the kayak and then followed the river upstream to get a clear view of the house. It takes about fifty strokes to reach the perfect viewing spot on the Sturgeon River. Looking up from the river the house appeared to be tucked within the slopes of a lush green mountain. The house seemed to be framed by trees and dappled with sunlight filtering through. A light breeze made the hot 29 degrees Celsius sunshine feel very comfortable. I let one hand slip into the water and enjoyed the sheer natural beauty surrounding us.

It took a lot of hard labour but by the afternoon of July 17th things looked great – the job was done by three o'clock that afternoon. The three of them had helped nature show off her inherent beauty. Majestic trees swayed in the breeze unencumbered by overgrown weeds. Sunshine reached the forest floor in every direction making the wild purple trillium plants very happy.

Ray had left an hour or so ago and I decided to go out and putter around my vegetable garden. Sasha was underfoot as always, hoping for a bite of vegetables. Suddenly, the wind felt different, almost solid. There was a subtle shift in the atmosphere. Everything seemed to go quiet. Sasha took off for the garage with her tail between her legs. The wind took on a menacing aura – I looked northwest and the sky was very dark – it looked odd, with grey swirls.

I decided it was time to go in the house. I took two pepper plants and stuck them in the garage, while shouting at Sasha to come with me. I ran back to get the okra plant, but the pot was too heavy to lift. I closed the greenhouse doors, picked Sahsa up, as she refused to leave the garage and headed home. At the door, I yelled at Ric that there seemed to be a strange weather pattern blowing in fast.

"The power went out a while back," Ric retorted.

"I am not surprised; the wind has picked up and does not feel right. The skies to the north are very dark," My tone had an uncharacteristically high note that expressed inner panic.

"Should I get the generator going or wait until the storm passes?" Ric asked. We had a small discussion and decided that it was prudent to get it going.

I stood looking out the kitchen window as the dark skies approached, obliterating the blue summer sky. The wind was howling through the house as all our windows were open. As it gushed through the rooms, papers began to fly. The trees bent over facing south and almost touching the ground. I ran to the north facing bathrooms to fasten the windows. The fury of the wind could be felt in the house as the outside went dark. I shut what I could as I ran from room to room, my fear for our safety increasing.

"Get down to the basement now," I heard Ric yelling at the top of the stairs. "Leave everything, I have Sasha," he cried.

"Hurry!" I could hear the fear in his voice.

As I left the bedroom, running towards the basement door, I saw the river was churning, boiling as it were. I could taste my fear as the witches lines from Shakespeare's play Macbeth popped in my mind:

"Double, double toil and trouble.
Fire burn, and cauldron bubble."

In total darkness, the three of us sat huddled together in the basement. Sasha trembled uncontrollably in my arms. We could hear loud crashes and ugly sounds. We could hear the rain hammering at the basement windows, the wind howling and trees breaking. My mouth felt dry, while my heart beat painfully against my chest. Over and over again I was thankful that we were sharing this moment. If this is the end, I thought, I want us to go together. I kept thinking that the house is going to be swept away in the wind. It seemed like hours, but it was just minutes, when the fury of the wind abated. The air was filled with thunder and the lighting broke the sheer darkness of the basement.

I got up and checked the phones – dead – no dial tone. Ric went upstairs to investigate. He came back after a few minutes, his skin pale white. In all the years that we have been together I have never seen him look so white – not even when he has been in pain nor after a long winter with minimal exposure to the sun.

"What has happened?" I whispered.

"Utter devastation outside," Ric said sadly.

"The house…." I was too stricken to finish the thought.

"Thank God, the house seems intact, but every window that I looked out of showed trees down. "It is a mess out there!"

Miraculously, the only damage to our house was a small dent in one eavestrough where a tree grazed it on the way down. In all forty beautiful old trees came down around the house–some fell just a foot away. Despite the passage of time I have not found the answer, "how did the house survive?" Ric has figurines and a beautiful statue of Buddha nestled amongst the trees on the riverside. Trees snapped, branches came down and a huge old tree was completely uprooted, but not one of the figurines was damaged.

Every year Ric stores the figurines in the garage through the harsh winters and then brings them out late in the spring. Every summer, I gaze into the eyes of Buddha and wonder what forces were at play that day.

Symbiotic Relationships

Have you ever wondered how we know that we have met our 'soul-mate' or life partner? Have you ever thought about how we know when the relationship is going to work? I have. In those quiet moments when I seemingly am doing nothing, my brain jumps from one thought to the other. I wonder about destiny and life choices. What makes us complete and what creates strife within? Mostly I have no answers or revelations – I just send questions out into the universe.

As I wrote this chapter, I realized that Ric and I have entered the twenty-fifth year of our relationship. We have spent the majority of that time together – we started our business soon after we met. It is not easy to work and play together. Yet we would not change anything at all. I never wanted a 'girls only' vacation, I never felt like going out for dinner with just some special friends. It has always been about the two of us enjoying life in all its intensity as a couple.

Someone commented that Ric and I must enjoy the same hobbies and activities since we have no other friends. That comment is what led me to think about our relationship. I realized that we cherish many similar things – like good food, cooking, peace and the antics of our dog. Yet we are two very dissimilar people.

Ric loves background music throughout the day – jazz, blues, classical, instrumental, oriental – a vast variety. I on the other hand can leave the music alone for the most part. I cannot imagine even one day without a book in my hand. He like puzzles, newspapers and crosswords. I like to kayak, he likes to canoe. He likes driving; I do it as a necessity. I like to fret over bank balances, investments and taxes; he takes them in his stride.

He is a dreamer and I am a worrier. He is a thinker and I leap in. He is a man of few words in a social setting and I chatter away. I avoid shopping at all costs and he does it with grace. I hate spending money; he sees it as a means to an end. He likes watching television and I like staring at the water. Yet our two halves make us whole. The essence of us lies in the symbiotic nature of our relationship. While being different, we are interdependent.

The key in our world has been respect and acceptance. If we had competing spirits, they were lost early on. Neither tries to change the other. There is no such thing as the perfect match, where each is exactly the same as the other. Respect comes from understanding. Acceptance leads to a mutually beneficial relationship.

Love is an elusive sentiment. It embodies caring and sacrifice. It is what binds two different people to follow the same path in life. It is the taste of fear when faced with danger. It is what makes us strong when faced with adversity. It can be expressed through romantic gestures, flowers, gifts and candlelight but its truth is felt with every breath we take. Every action, every moment while awake or asleep is an equally powerful expression of true love.

Those dark moments that life brings us, threats to our wellbeing become lighter when shared in love. With love at our side every challenge helps us grow stronger. When those tears fall, as they must in life, the other half is there to dry them. Life's journey is worthwhile because we have each other.

In good times the joy is intensified and in bad times the burden is lighter. Emerging from a dark basement, after cowering together in fear to face a huge cleanup and seven days without hydro or phones and the shutdown of our North America wide business was just another test that the school of life sent us. Ric took it as a personal challenge to show off his barbequing skills. The cast iron pans and skillets became our friends—hash browns, bacon and eggs greeted each morning.

"Since there is nothing we can do about the business, there is not much point in fretting," Ric would remind me as he would fire up the Big Green Egg charcoal barbeque to prepare dinner. Nature forced us to take a vacation. We did not miss a beat – I made rice on the propane barbeque, curried chicken and many other favourites. Ric perfected the art of stabilizing the temperature on the charcoal barbeque to such a level that we were able to bake fresh yeast breads through the blackout.

The generator kept the well pump in business and we had running water in the house.

When I started to worry about our clients not getting service, he would tell me to think of it all as a great adventure, as he'd drive us to the pay phone in Field so I could remotely access our business voice mail and return calls. We spent countless hours outdoors clearing up the mess, with the help of a local lumberjack named Leo. Hours after Ric and his crew had prettied up our landscape, nature roughed it up, while giving us forty beautiful trees that provided firewood for many winters to come.

"Things happen for a reason and at that moment the reason may seem obscure; rest assured there is a reason," is a mantra that goes on in my head. How else can one get through life's curve balls? I have a strong belief that events, however bad they may seem, have a purpose in our lives and the purpose is mostly for our own good.

Before we purchased the house in Field, we made sure that West Nipissing had a hospital, and of course a public library. After we made the move we discovered that none of the doctors were accepting new patients. Neither of us was too concerned as it was not normal for us to get sick or need a physician. We spoke to our family doctor in Toronto about staying with her until the circumstances changed. Ric had been a client of Dr. Rossiter's for over thirty years and she agreed to keep our files open.

Our first winter at Kashmir Acres presented the first 'health-challenge.' Ric has had ongoing issues with his back, after hurting it lifting heavy boxes years ago. On a cold afternoon in February he leaned over to play with Sasha while sitting by the fireplace and he felt a tug in his lower back. When he straightened up and tried to stand, he knew he was in trouble. The next few days were tough. He is the strong, independent type, who will suffer in silence. He is quick to help others but will not ask for help when he needs it. We argued and I fretted. Finally, we called Dr. Rossiter in Toronto, who diagnosed the problem over the phone and sent a prescription to a pharmacy in Sturgeon Falls.

Love is patience, understanding and stifling anger! Love is not screaming at each other and throwing things in frustration. Ric's back was in such bad shape by this time, there was no way he could drive to Sturgeon Falls to pick-up the medicine. I did not drive at all–Toronto had provided me with mobility through its transit system. Anywhere I needed to go, the subway, street cars or buses provided door-to-door service. A few months after we moved north, both our families used to admonish me with, "You have to learn to drive. You cannot live in the country without the ability to drive!" I ignored the voices and carried on with life.

We had to get a taxi to bring us the medicines and take me grocery shopping. It was an expensive proposition but we had no choice. Sadly, Ric did not get better. Soon he was lying in bed in agony. I made soup and tried to lift his head enough for him to swallow the broth, but that was becoming increasingly difficult. Dr. Rossiter wanted me to get him to the hospital, but my darling, stubborn husband refused to go. Did I say love is all about patience and not throttling your loved ones when they are being extremely stubborn?

I lay beside Ric, hearing his soft moans. His breathing was labored as the slightest movement caused his back to spasm – each spasm made him scream in agony. I felt a deep sense of helplessness. I felt the pain in my bones. I tasted the salt of my tears as I tried to keep still. The night outside was dark, but the light from the stars reflected off the snow. It was midnight and we were both awake, each pretending to be asleep. Loud, sharp and clear the hoot of an owl penetrated the house. I got up and looked outside our bedroom window, but saw nothing other than the night. The owl continued its mournful song all night long, never tiring and never stopping, as we lay listening. The sound of the owl evoked strong emotions in both of us. I felt the hand of a guiding spirit as the burdens of the last few days left my soul. The hooting of the owl provided solace and a certainty that change was on its way. As the sun came up on the eastern horizon, Ric whispered, "Call an ambulance, please!"— when I failed to reach him, my favourite bird broke through.

While our marriage vows did not incorporate the traditional, "Will you love him, comfort him, honour and keep him in sickness and in health," over the years the lines have echoed in my head many a time. Through some of my own health scares, I am sure Ric has had the same thoughts.

The owl has never reappeared in our lives, even though we live in the country surrounded by forests and water. Its one powerful interaction with us was the harbinger of change. The wisdom of its unknown message in a language foreign to us led us on a path peppered with life's magic.

Sowing "Future" Seeds

"What would you like for your fiftieth birthday?" Ric asked as we carried crates of potatoes to the cold cellar. The harvest had been good and we have lots of potatoes. Beautiful round Yukon Gold potatoes, oblong shaped light-skinned Shepodies and the traditional baking variety Russet Burbank.

Huffing and puffing as we went up and down the steep steps to the basement cellar, I said, "Visit your mother and an iPad!" The year I turned fifty, Ric's mom was in long-term care and just a few years shy of her ninetieth birthday. She and I had been best friends in our younger years. We gossiped, we cooked, we shopped, we cried, we giggled and we laughed.

Every time I reflect on the years gone by, I realize that things have changed so much. My grandfather was born in 1897 and he passed away in the 1990's, after I moved to Canada. I grew up in an era where educated people may have had access to a typewriter. I still remember the 'ping' of the machine when it reached the end of a line of text and a lever was pushed to get the mechanism to move to the next line. My early writing skills were honed on a piece of slate with white chalk.

I became a young professional in a time where there were rotary phones, telex machines, telegrams and a 'pager' to stay connected to the office. I got an iPad 2 for my fiftieth birthday – a big leap for us. Admittedly, for the first year or more it was used like an e-reader, but since then it has grown to include an 'app' for the weather network, Facebook and TSN.

While I continue to avoid getting sucked into the 24-7 world of social media and breaking news, I am constantly amazed at the ease with which the world of information has become one with the human conscience. I watch people tapping at flat handheld devices at all times: at home, in meetings, at the restaurant, while walking, while talking, while eating and I think to myself, "When does the mind rest?"

A decade after we met the owl I passed my G Class Driver's test. It took a while, but it got done. I had to go to North Bay for the road test, which is well outside my comfort zone – too many people and too much traffic. The city has a population of just under 54,000 people—approximately the number of people that can attend a concert in the former Skydome in Toronto.

Soon after we moved to Kashmir Acres we fell into a nightly routine. During the cold nights of winter, we'd sit in front of a blazing fire and relax before heading to bed. Through the other three seasons, we'd sit on the riverside patio letting the night sounds and the chirping of insects soothe us. It has become a welcome nightly ritual. It is our moment to solve the world's problems and create memories. It is a time to reflect, to give thanks and to strengthen our friendship.

It was on a cold night in February, our sixth winter at Kashmir Acres. I had just returned from attending an evening session at the Near North Garden Club in Sturgeon Falls. Since I did not drive, Carole Anne a member of the club and a neighbour to the north, offered to take me to the event. They had invited me to share my novice experiences with gardening at their February meeting. It was a windy evening with heavy snow. As always, it never ceases to amaze me how dedicated gardeners are to their favourite past-time. A lot of members showed up and it was a great exchange.

"How did the meeting go?" Ric asked as we basked in front of the fire, later that night.

"It was great. I got over my nervousness and the presentation was well received," I said as I enjoyed a snack Ric had made for me.

"Will you be joining the club?" Ric said softly, as he got up to add another log in the fire.

"I am not sure – they were all really nice but you know how I feel about groups of people!" I said with a shrug. "It's not easy – I never feel comfortable."

"Would you like a glass of wine?" Ric asked with a smile, knowing I would not refuse. As he went to pour us some, my mind wandered back to the meeting. It was my first speaking engagement on the topic of gardening and my first garden club meeting. It was nice sitting with like-minded souls for a few hours, but—"

"So tell me all about it," Ric's voice interrupted my musings.

"The meeting began with their normal order of business, including a report from the Treasurer. It appears they are not attracting new members and there was a discussion around this topic. They bandied around ideas like a free membership for a year if an existing member brought in a new member. Everything seemed very short-term," I remarked.

"What were you thinking?" Ric said, as he got up to turn down a few lights and lower the volume on the CD player.

Taking a sip of wine I said with a shrug, "I am not sure. Oh! I liked some of the ideas, but I feel like the problem runs deeper than just a drop in membership."

We sat in silence for a while, enjoying the music and the wine. I had this nagging feeling that somewhere in the recesses of my brain there was a thought just waiting to pop out. Sometimes the harder I try to focus on an elusive idea the further away it moves.

"Why do you think they are not attracting new members?" Ric said.

"Uhm! There were no young people at the meeting," I said. "That may be the key to the problem."

"Do you think it is because people are not interested in gardening?" Ric asked. "Could that be the cause?"

"Makes sense, now that you mention it. It would explain why they are not attracting new members. The long-term solution would be to get people excited about growing things. Once people engage in outdoor activities, like gardening, they are going to want to share ideas. Look how many online garden forums I joined as we began our journey with growing vegetables!" I exclaimed. I remember signing up to all kinds of online sources of information and exchange. I had and continue to have questions. The more I learn, the more I don't know – it is like going in circles but in a nice way.

"So why don't you write about it?" Once again, Ric interrupted my thoughts.

"Write about what?" I said somewhat irritated. Sometimes I am not sure where Ric goes with his comments. There are times when we are so attuned to each other's thoughts, we can complete sentences and ideas and then there are moments like these.

"Our gardening adventures, of course!" Ric exclaimed with a self-satisfied smile.

My annoyance was beginning to show as I retorted sharply, "And how is that going to help?"

"If two city-dwellers like us, who work full-time, could learn to grow vegetables, so can others around us!" He has this huge grin on his face and he was strutting around in front of the fireplace, acting like he had solved this problem.

"I still don't see what you see," I said morosely. Actually I was feeling decidedly grumpy and tired. The evening high was hitting a low – I had been running on adrenalin throughout the garden club meeting and presentation.

"Look, think about it – people will read about our misadventures and through all the mistakes we will share our final success. Don't you love all the herbs and vegetables we grow!" Ric exclaimed, looking smug.

I have to give him credit for persisting. I could see so many holes in his theory, I was starting to think we should go to bed and let this conversation rest. On the other hand, we could keep at it and probably we'd end up in some big argument. Suddenly, I pinpointed the flaw.

"Where would we write all this good stuff?" I demanded with a smirk.

"In the newspaper of course," he replied matter-of-factly.

I just looked at my darling husband, wondering if he had lost his marbles.

"You are always scribbling in that diary of yours, why not put the fingers to good use – write in the newspaper!" he said writing in the air with a flourish.

"Write in the newspaper?" I squeaked. "How?"

Right from the very beginning our relationship was based on a solutions-driven approach. In business Ric used to tell the team not to come to him with problems, but with solutions. The strategy worked well and the staff learned to think. Problem solving skills in business and at home are essential for growth. In no time we came up with a simple plan. We began with pitching the idea to Carole Anne. She liked it very much, especially since we were volunteering to do the writing. Through some discussion, Carole Anne and I decided we would approach a local paper. We did, but were met with no response.

"Too bad," I told Ric a few weeks later. "I had really hoped we could get something going before the end of March but the paper did not call back."

"Why don't you give the Nugget a call?" Ric suggested. "It is not like you to give up so easily. Besides you have already written sample articles – somebody other than me should read them."

"If the local paper did not respond, why would one out of North Bay – their circulation is about ten times more." I remarked dejectedly.

"Well you won't know until you ask!" Ric replied nodding his head wisely.

Taking his advice, I sent a short letter by email to the "then-Managing Editor, Steve Hardy." Within an extremely short time he emailed back with a request for some samples of the proposed column. He saw a fit with their publication, Community Voices. Dawn Clarke looked after that publication and in no time we were in communication about the columns. In less than four weeks from initial contact, the first 'Northern Vegetables' column appeared in the Friday, March 27, 2009 edition of Community Voices.

It began with the line: "The birds have been very active this winter at the feeders."

The first reader communication arrived by email on April 5, 2009. Fleur's first line read: "I've been enjoying reading your articles in Community Voices over the past couple of weeks."

We both were elated with the response from the readers. Our first reaction was one of wonder, "Wow! Somebody actually read it and took the time to respond." More than five years later, we get regular emails, telephone messages and hand written notes. Some have questions, many share their gardening knowledge, others send seeds but each one encourages and inspires me to keep writing, 'Northern Vegetables,' week after week.

THEN AND NOW

The breeze held the promise of spring with a hint of lingering winter. As I walked back to the house from 'the point' – the spot where we have our river dock in the summer – I found it hard to believe it was the end of April. It had been a bitterly cold and long winter. Temperatures fell below minus forty degrees Fahrenheit a few times and we had several feet of snow. Even now, as I make my way back, I can see large patches of snow that is yet to melt. The Sturgeon River is running high and flowing fast as it accepts the melting snow.

All winter we watched the deer struggle in the deep snow. We had six at a time, wandering along the edges of our land, seeking food. The birds that stay with us over the winter were constant companions, complaining loudly if the feeders were empty for even a moment. Pretty Blue Jays, graceful woodpeckers and delicate song birds, living in harmony. I made my way up the tiny hill and as I walked past the rhubarb patch I noticed tiny red growth – the first to appear every spring.

Ric and Sasha came out to greet me. For an old dog, she still has a spring in her step when she gets excited. Ric is aging gracefully, battling aches and pains that seem synonymous with advancing years. "How was your walk?"

"Wonderful! I was a bit cold, but it was great not having to don on my snowshoes. You can quit worrying about the dock; it is tied to two trees and seems pretty secure. Even if we see shore erosion, I think the trees are pretty safe – they should survive the spring flooding." I reassured him, underestimating the power of Mother Nature. The warmth of the house was welcoming and a nice break from the cold wind.

"I saw deer scat in many places. There was another pile along the path that was light brown, about an inch long and a quarter inch or so in diameter." I decided to warm up a small bowl of soup and take it into the great room. As I turned, I noticed the smile on Ric's face, humour glinting in his eyes and then he burst out laughing.

"What's so funny?" I demanded, settling down on my favourite spot on the couch.

"I just had a flashback to another time." Ric made himself comfortable in his favorite chair by the fireplace. "You would leave the office to go to the Bank of Montreal on Bloor Street. On your return you'd come into my office and invariably there would be a discussion of what was going on in the area."

As I transported back in time, I remembered that when I went to the bank to make deposits, I took different routes to get some exercise. Sometimes I'd go straight down Yonge Street, past The Hudson's Bay store at the corner of Yonge and Bloor Streets. Our business bank was located in the Manulife Centre on Bloor Street, across from the prestigious Holt Renfrew store. Other times, I'd make my way through Yorkville or Hazleton Lanes. If I really wanted to get a good walk in, I'd go up to Avenue Road and make my way back past the Chapters-Indigo store on Bloor Street. Sometimes—

Ric's voice interrupted my thoughts. "You would come in to my office and tell me that Holt Renfrew has a sale on or that you had to check out Jones New York at The Bay because they had a person at the corner of Bay and Bloor handing out 25% off cards or—."

Swallowing a mouthful of hot soup, I joined in the laughter and let the memories flood back. "What a difference is perspective, from that walk to this walk. Now I am talking about 'animal poop.' Though I think the distance I travelled to the bank and back is about the same to our point, don't you think?" I asked Ric.

"For sure, it may be a bit more. If you went up our driveway, then walk east to the far field and then along the forest's edge to the trail that leads to the point, I think that would easily be the distance from our office to Avenue Road, then back to Bloor Street and up Yonge" Ric remarked as he mentally mapped out the distance and made the comparison.

"Oh! I almost forgot, the ice over the pond is gone and looks like the ducks are back in it." For many years the ducks have found a safe place in this little natural pond. It is surrounded by tall trees and there is a natural trail on opposite banks where the beaver come up from the river. Along the banks of the pond, hidden by reeds and tall grass, partridge nest. Every spring as the ducks return to the river, we see a few flying directly over our point, close to the pond. Eventually a few make the pond their home until it is time for them to leave us.

"QUACK, quack, quack," Ric mimicked the call of the ducks. "Do you remember?" His mischievous smile gave away the answer. It is amazing how much a human expression can convey when we are at ease. I have always enjoyed reading people. Silently observing non-verbal signals and picking up clues and discrepancies that negate the spoken word. Most of us maintain a subtle shield that our subconscious throws out when we are in public or away from our comfort zone. When I have the opportunity to interact with the same people overtime, the non-verbal signals convey far more than the words.

This time Ric had travelled back to a lovely little cottage nestled by the shores of a bay off the Atlantic Ocean. "Halifax?" I asked, as memories of salty breezes and fish assailed my senses. In my early twenties, while living in Kenya, Africa, I had secured a marketing contract for a resort on the Indian Ocean in Mombasa and the owner's dry-cleaning business in Nairobi. It was my first large contract. The campaign was a one-person deal – I took the photographs for the brochures, wrote content, completed layouts, planned the unveiling and advertising campaigns. I rebranded the dry cleaning business and created the required promotional strategy. It was a time full of energy, deadlines, anxiety, exhilaration, delicious seafood, ocean breezes and beer. There is no mistaking the smell of the ocean and all its mysteries.

"Yes, Halifax!" Ric replied giving me a salute for getting it right.

Business in Toronto was booming and we were feeling both the pleasure of money flowing in and the pain of dealing with the resulting pace. We both knew we were at a breaking point and needed to recharge our batteries. A few years before, while Ric was the Human Resources Manager for Bata Canada he had to travel to Nova Scotia on business. I had been working at a travel agency and had earned a free ticket to fly anywhere in Canada. I decided to tag along. It was in November and even though it was a cold and wet experience we both really enjoyed our time on the east coast. We decided to return to the beautiful province of Nova Scotia for a break from the grind of Toronto.

Our stay was short and sweet. The little cottage was perfect – just a bit isolated, on the water and it had a barbecue – the perfect setting for two urbanites living in a penthouse condominium. We had rented a car at the airport and took to travelling to tiny villages. We found a lobster farm where the catch of the day would come in early in the morning. It became our favourite place to get fresh seafood daily. Ric was in barbecue heaven and I knew that one day, when we had our dream home, he would want a barbecue before anything else.

On our first day at the cottage, I was inside unpacking and Ric was outside, I could hear this strange noise. It was loud and discordant but it sounded like Ric's deep voice. I rushed out, fearing that he had hurt himself, only to be greeted by the oddest sight. Ric was sitting on the steps, leaning forward and just straight ahead a bit to the right was a duck looking straight at him. I watched in wonder as it would quack and Ric would reply. It carried on this conversation with Ric for a while, before taking off. To my utter amazement, every day that we were at the cottage the duck retuned and sat by the stairs 'quacking' with Ric. Ric carried that particular language back with him and often as the summer sun goes down at Kashmir Acres, I can hear him quacking with the ducks on the river.

Often as I stride toward an unknown destination at Kashmir Acres, moments from the past flash before my eye. The mind makes remarkable associations and replays vivid scenes that exemplify the power of our brain cells. Despite being away from the break-neck speed of Toronto for more than a decade, I have not lost my purposeful and fast gait. I do not stroll languidly through the fields – I move with speed. On a sunny day, as I headed to our vegetable patch, my stride startled a beautiful Northern Flicker from its ant-hunt. As it took off, a flash of golden feathers, the beautiful red stripe on the back of its head caught my eye and transported me back to Joso's Restaurant on Davenport Road in Toronto.

A landmark since the sixties, Joso's restaurant was a favourite celebration spot for Ric and I. Its eclectic décor, unusual style and original art made it perfect for us. Bright colours, with a predominance of red make it a very bold and unique restaurant experience. Fresh seafood, simple and clean flavours were especially appealing to our pallet. Ric had been going there well before he met me. Joso and his son Leo were always there to greet guests. We were recognized as regulars, even though we made our way to the restaurant only once every few months.

Joso's saw its share of visiting celebrities and dignitaries – Nana Mouskouri, Harry Belafonte, Gordon Lightfoot, Joni Mitchell, Jose Feliciano, Liberace, Anne Murray to name a few. It was not unusual to be dining at Joso's and be sitting across from a famous person. The Northern Flicker's bright red neck colour had the power to bring back so much so fast. I recall the evening we took a business colleague, Witold and his wife, to dinner at Joso's. Typical of a first time guest they were fascinated by the ambience and the art. We were escorted to a table upstairs and had just made our wine selections when the owner's son Leo came to Ric. He was very apologetic and asked if we would allow them to move our party to the table right next to this one. Apparently, Mel Brooks had arrived and our table was his favourite spot in the restaurant. And we spent the rest of the occasion right next to Mel Brooks, his wife Anne Bancroft and their guests.

A flash of white brought me back to the present, just in time to see a deer disappear into the bush at the far end of our property. Like a broken record, Ric and I keep asking each other, "Any regrets?" or "Do you miss Toronto?" or "Is this too much for us?" Frankly, neither of us can imagine returning to the life we had in Toronto. Sure we exchanged the all-pervasive sounds of traffic with the insistent call of birds; we gave up the constant screech of sirens for the lone call of the wolf; we left the drunken cries of late night revelers behind, only to be faced by the absolute silence of a dark northern night. We left Toronto and its over two million people for the village of Field – population just over six hundred.

Tears of Joy

The gentle rain cooled my skin as I worked in the garden on a hot July day. The soft mist soothed the parched earth and the plants leaned into it, seemingly soaking in every drop into their pores. Just over a decade had passed since we left the city behind. My fingers ached from rescuing the rows of onions from the all-pervasive grass and weed. Over the years I had learned that any piece of weed left in the ground would come back with a vengeance. The only way to make my efforts count was to remove every part of the grass and weed from the ground.

My eyes drifted toward the river and I watched the rain create mystical patterns on the water's surface – a language all of its own. I fancied I could read the future in that script, if I squinted hard enough, I would see some words form. Salty tears flowed and mixed in with the gentle rain. I felt the heavy shroud of sadness surround me like a cloak. The soulful call of the loon filled the air around me and like the swollen river the tears poured out of my eyes.

Memories flooded back. I remember a similar ache inside the day Ric trapped the resident ground hog and took it away. It looked at me with huge eyes that seemed to reproach our actions. It made me feel guilty for asking Ric to take it away. In that moment as I looked into its caged eyes, I forgot that it had damaged my gardens one too many times.

The haunting cry of our resident loon filled the air, reminding me that things happen for a reason. The ground hog probably made itself a bigger and better home away from us. Where there is life, there is purpose. We live in harmony with all creatures, great and small. Some we relocated, some we rescued and a few we helped along. Different moments, different sounds taught us that all living beings should be respected and no matter how big or small, sometimes a helping hand is most welcome.

A loud thud on a cold wintery morning meant that a little bird had hit one of our windows. The knowledge that it would not survive outside in the minus thirty degrees Celsius temperatures spurred both of us into action. I ran to bring it in, while Ric created a makeshift bed in a box. The tiny helpless bird weighed next to nothing. I could barely feel its heartbeat as it lay nestled in my hands. I spoke to it softly promising that it will be fine when it woke up. While Ric and I wondered what to do next, the little bird came to and looked at both of us as if it wanted to say, "What do you think you are doing?" The tears of relief and happiness that moistened our eyes as we released it outside and saw it fly away and created another unforgettable moment.

The words on the river's surface became clear as the tears slowed down – 'nature commands all' it said. I understood the root of my sadness – the power of the river to give and to take away at its whim. For a decade we had enjoyed its bounty and its benevolence – fresh fish caught off our river dock, relaxing canoe and kayak rides. Hours spent watching river traffic – the beavers, otters, ducks, geese, mergansers, herons, loons, belted kingfishers, beautiful fox, deer and moose.

This year, after a long harsh and snowy winter, the river broke through in all its placid glory. Only below the mirror like surface a ferocious current was at work. The river rose to new heights flooding the lower reaches of our land. The two natural ponds that provide a safe haven for water fowl all summer spread out and became one with mighty river. After running high for weeks as the snow melted and then the rains came, the river finally started to recede. The levels returned to near normal too fast.

With the precision of a surgeon, much like the time that I underwent surgery to remove a 'dreaded lump' and a suspicious mass, the river carved out chunks of the land. Swathes of land, along with dozens of healthy trees floated down river. Our handsome river dock became a casualty of the river's strength. More tears washed away in the rain as I realized that I had lost my kayak launching site and my fishing hole. The natural beaches had disappeared leaving sheer drops to the river's surface. The summer loomed without a chance to dip into the water.

A clap of thunder close by signaled it was time to seek shelter and shake off the blues—after all the surgically removed lumps were cancer-free. In that moment as I ran toward the house, I felt the shroud of darkness leave me and lightness permeate my soul. Eventually, the scales of life create a balance. When there are tears, surely laughter will follow. After all, *it's OK to laugh in the garden.*